in the SUN

Celtic's Wonder Year of 1966/67

John TRAYNOR & Tony GRIFFIN

A SEASON IN THE SUN, Celtic's Wonder Year of 1966/67 was written by John Traynor and Tony Griffin.

The authors are indebted to Jim and Paul Traynor for invaluable assistance in drafting the manuscript.

First published 1992 by Lion Books.

British Library Cataloguing-in-Publication Data.
A catalogue record for this book is available from the British Library.

ISBN 0 9520458 0 X

Photographs Courtesy of Evening Times/Herald.
Typesetting and Page Make-up by Trinity Typesetting, Edinburgh
Origination by Reprolink, Dunfermline
Cover Concept by Douglas G. Russell.

Printed in Scotland by Allander Litho, Edinburgh.

Prologue

'It is up to us, to everyone at Celtic Park now, to build up our own legends. We don't want to live with history, to be compared to legends of the past. We must make *new* legends and our League Championship win is the first step towards doing that.'

Jock Stein, Monday 9th May, 1966, two days after the clinching of Celtic's first League Championship in twelve years. The rest *is* legend.

Thanks to all who made this possible

Contents

Introduction

If, as the old adage asserts, all roads lead to Rome, then in the early weeks of May, 1967 a massive diversion must have been in operation. For in those heady days, when the spirit of The Celtic Football Club was on the move, all roads led inexorably, not to the 'Eternal City' but to Lisbon, Portugal, where *The Famous Glasgow Celtic* had a date with destiny. Having swept all before them throughout a breathtaking season, the expansive National Stadium in that historic capital was to be the venue for Celtic's greatest triumph to date, which would conclude another indelible chapter in a history littered with unique achievements.

On 25th May, 1967, Celtic became not only the first *Scottish* but the first *British* and indeed, the first *non-Latin* club to win the European Champions' Cup, following in the footsteps of the incomparable Real Madrid, whose five successive victories from the tournament's inception in 1955/56 will probably never be equalled. The great Spanish club was immortalised in Scottish football history by the unforgettable Hampden final of 1960 against Eintracht Frankfurt, a match which etched such names as Di Stefano, Puskas and Gento forever into our national psyche. The mighty señors were also Celtic's immediate predecessors as European Champions, having lifted the trophy for a sixth time in a 2-1 victory over Partizan Belgrade in 1966.

The other former champions were the 'Eagles' of Benfica (1961,1962), A.C.Milan (1963) and their great local rivals, Internazionale, who, under the dead hand of coach Helenio Herrera, had imposed the sterile philosophy of *Catenaccio* on Europe in 1964 and 1965 and who were to be Celtic's Lisbon opponents. The picturesque Portuguese capital would prove to be a graveyard for the Italians' negative, defensive tactics, thoroughly discredited and dismantled by the storm of the Scots' cavalier attacking style, so reminiscent of those former Madrid maestros.

In addition to the historic *firsts* detailed above, Celtic were also the first team of genuine home nationality to conquer Europe. All who had gone before were of cosmopolitan make-up, often having plundered the football world in search of success. Not so Celtic! The eleven who aspired to soccer immortality that day were as Scottish as 'the cratur', truly *Lisbon Lions Rampant.*

Furthermore, though in a somewhat more fanciful vein, 1967 was the first and probably the only time the Champions' Cup would be won by *fans*. For who can doubt that the magnificent travelling support, who had won over the locals and converted them to the Celtic cause long before a ball was kicked, as well as the frustrated thousands watching at home, made every tackle, stroked every pass, cut out every dangerous cross and fired in every shot along with their heroes? Or who would deny that the young men privileged to wear the hoops that day and who stunned their more elegant megastar rivals with an impromptu rendition of *The Celtic Song* on the long walk to the pitch, were, in a very special sense, Celtic supporters?

Over the years Celtic have specialised in records and *one- offs,* setting standards and chalking up sometimes unlikely victories which either never *could* or at any rate probably never *would* be repeated, far less surpassed (except, perhaps, by some future Celtic side!).

Six consecutive League Championships from 1904/05 to 1909/10 are commemorated by a splendid shield which has pride of place on the Board Room wall in the heart of Celtic Park. Although no-one seriously suspected it at the time, the 1966/67 title was to be the second in an exhilarating charge to nine straight Championships, easily eclipsing even that great sequence of sixty years earlier.... but sadly, not so graciously marked for posterity by the contemporaries of the Celtic of the 'sixties and 'seventies.

Five glittering prizes, the envy of the greatest clubs in the land, adorn the main trophy showcase, again in the Board Room, bearing proud testimony to the Celtic tradition of rising to the great occasion. Won outright and held on a permanent basis, these epic trophies are woven into the very fabric of The Celtic Football Club, forever charting the high points of a wondrous, sprawling football saga.

Visitors to Celtic Park gaze in reverential awe at The Glasgow Exhibition Cup (1902), The Empire Exhibition Trophy (1938), The Victory in Europe Cup (1945), The St Mungo Cup (1951) and The Coronation Cup (1953), each redolent of historic significance, conjuring up images of legendary characters and evoking memories of heroic deeds in stirring competition. The stories of these 'landmark' trophies form a fascinating Appendix to this story and place it in historical perspective.

Read on, then and bathe awhile in the comforting warmth of *A Season in the Sun.*

Photograph courtesy of Evening Times/Herald

Dressing room celebrations after clinching the League Championship for the first time in twelve years, Fir Park, Motherwell, 7th May, 1966.

Chapter One

Seeds of Glory: The American Dream Tour

Time has not dulled the memory, even with the passage of more than a quarter of a century. The date was 7th May, 1966, the place, Fir Park, Motherwell and the occasion, the clinching of Celtic's first Scottish League Championship in twelve long years. In truth, the flag had been effectively won the previous Wednesday evening by dint of a 2-1 home win over Dunfermline Athletic, which had meant that only a 4-0 defeat, or worse, by Motherwell could have taken the title to Ibrox on *goal average* (the curious forerunner of today's *goal difference*). In the event, Bobby Lennox's last-minute conversion of Jim Craig's cut-back from the bye-line ensured that the final margin of Celtic's victory was a comfortable two points.

Celtic fans had flocked confidently to Motherwell in their thousands to celebrate a famous triumph and the persistant recollection is of a row of ecstatic supporters, totally oblivious to peril, acclaiming their heroes from the roof of the Fir Park enclosure as the team took a bow in the centre circle. Such was the determination of this section of the 'faithful' to witness the affirmation of Celtic's re-emergence as *the* power in Scottish football, they were prepared to risk life and limb just to *be* there.

The following week, a party of Celtic players and officials set off on a tour of Bermuda, U.S.A. and Canada. This was a well-trodden path, following on from the historic tours of 1931 and 1951 and was to comprise eleven games in the course of a month, ranging from 'shooting practice' against local select sides to serious competitive matches involving other touring European clubs, Tottenham Hotspur, Bayern Munich and Bologna. The tour was partly a deserved reward for a job well done in the season just past (1965/66). Not only had Celtic ended the League Championship famine, inflicting in the process a memorable 5-1 defeat on Rangers at Celtic Park on 3rd January, 1966, they had also lifted the League Cup, dumping Rangers 2-1 in the final, a result which

Photograph courtesy of Evening Times/Herald

Jock Stein always believed his players should come first and typically stays in the background as most of the party poses for photographers at Celtic Park prior to setting off on the 'American Dream Tour.' The line-up is (left to right): Charlie Gallagher, Steve Chalmers, Bobby Murdoch, Bobby Lennox, Willie O'Neill, Billy McNeill, Jimmy Johnstone, Frank McCarron, Ian Young, Bertie Auld, Ronnie Simpson (crouching), Joe McBride, John Cushley and John Fallon.

convinced many, however reluctantly in some cases, of a definite shift in power from Copland Road to Kerrydale Street. And although the Scottish Cup Final, lost 1-0 after a replay, afforded a measure of consolation to the men from Govan, even that Rangers win had the unmistakable look of a 'last hurrah' about it. They were forced to

Photograph courtesy of Evening Times/Herald

Everyone looks more relaxed now as they board the aircraft. Although Jock Stein is holding the Westclox Trophy, it is not yet his as the selection has still to be made.

defend for most of the two games and typically in such circumstances, snatched victory only when the Celtic defence lost concentration near the end of the replay.

Reaching the semi-final of the European Cup Winners' Cup had been an outstanding performance and Celtic were only narrowly eliminated by Liverpool (2-0 at Anfield, having won the first leg 1-0 in Glasgow), courtesy of an appalling refereeing decision to disallow a last-minute strike by Bobby Lennox on grounds of offside, even though the mercurial forward had carried the ball past a defender to score. It may be over-charitable to the official to suggest that the 'Buzz-Bomb' was a victim of his own electrifying pace; and certainly Lennox's 'goal' would have taken Celtic through to a virtual home final at Hampden Park against Borussia Dortmund of the then *West* Germany. The Germans eventually beat Liverpool 2-1, but formidable as they undoubtedly were, could they have overcome a rampant Celtic in front of 134,000 partisan Scots? It is doubtful - but such speculation is, of course, intrinsically futile and history records that European glory would just have to wait.

The Celtic party had barely touched down in Bermuda when news came through that Jock Stein had been elected as Scotland's *Manager of the Year*, no great surprise it has to be said. One week later, though, came a less - predictable accolade, as even the English bowed to his supremacy to crown him *Westclox British Manager of the Year* and complete a momentous double for the 'Big Man'.

The tour itself progressed much as expected. On Friday, 13th May, the visit of Celtic proved appropriately unlucky for a Bermuda Select which was buried under an avalanche of goals. The new Scottish Champions won 10-1, with goals from Lennox (4), Auld (3), Gemmell (2) and captain Billy McNeill. Bermuda Young Men fared little better two days later, going down 7-0. The prolific Lennox this time settled for a 'hat-trick', galloping Tommy Gemmell grabbed another brace and Joe McBride weighed in with his first two goals of the tour, one from the penalty spot.

Of course, these opening matches, plus the first U.S. appearance, a 6-0 canter over New Jersey All Stars, had never been intended as anything other than a mere warm-up for the infinitely more demanding encounters which lay ahead, beginning with the first of three jousts with Spurs, in Toronto on 22nd May. Bobby Lennox maintained his remarkable scoring run, notching the only goal of the game to give Celtic the psychological edge of a winning start to this Scotland/ England mini-series.

Meanwhile, back home, the Scotland national side suffered what was then a *shock* 3-0 trouncing from Holland in a friendly international at Hampden Park. [Before the match, outspoken sportswriter of the time, Hugh Taylor, had written: 'Without Anglos, without Celtic players, who will be starting their American tour, this Scotland team should be good enough to beat Holland,hardly in the top grade of world ratings.' (Daily Record, Saturday 7th May, 1966.) How wrong can you be?] Due to the non-availability, for one reason or another, of regular 'exiles' such as Billy Bremner, Denis Law, Jim Baxter (then with Sunderland) and Charlie Cooke, the Scots line-up was an 'all-tartan' (home-based) one, containing four new caps, Pat Stanton and Jim Scott (both Hibernian), Dave Smith (Aberdeen) and Andy Penman (Dundee). A certain Willie Wallace of Hearts also played, but the undisputed star of the show was Holland's sparkling young left-winger, Piet Keizer, of Ajax Amsterdam, who was to go on to form a devastating left-side partnership at both club and international level with the legendary Johann Cruyff. The Dutch side that evening gave us a glimpse of the future. Though still at the drawing board stage in 1966, their embryonic concept of *Total Football,* which would revolutionise the European soccer scene, was there for all to see.

On another front, the Daily Record reported on 23rd May that former Parkhead kingpin, Charlie Tully, manager of Portadown in the Irish league, had made a bid to sign two fellow ex-Celts, John Divers and Jim Conway, whose successors in the hoops were to taste stiff opposition for the first time Stateside in the shape of Bologna, of Italy, with whom they drew 0-0 in New York on 27th May.

The party then briefly crossed the border back into Canada to dispense a merciful 11-0 pasting (*well, it was 9-0 at half-time!*) to a Hamilton Select in Toronto, with Murdoch (3), Lennox (4), McBride (2), Clark (pen.) and Gemmell doing the damage. Next up were C.Y.C. All Stars, who were given the treatment 6-1 in St Louis, Missouri, on 29th May. Chalmers, Lennox, McBride (2), Auld and Hughes ensured that the goals were neatly distributed across the forward line on this occasion.

The psychology of undertaking such an arduous tour in the wake of a heavy, albeit successful, domestic campaign was brilliantly simple. Jock Stein wanted to build on the achievements of the season just past by fusing the emerging talents of his young players into a unit capable of confronting the challenges which he sensed lay ahead. What better way to weld the team spirit he craved than the combinations of relaxation and discipline, recreation and competition, *va*cation and *vo*cation which this extended working holiday would inevitably produce? The players would live in each others' pockets for a solid month and would learn to cope with the tensions, both positive and negative, such proximity creates. They would experience the excitement of foreign travel - in many cases, for the first time - *together* and in the course of travelling that vast continent, partnerships and friendships would be forged and cemented which would later bear fruit both on and off the field. A perfect example of such liaisons is the improbable and enduring bond struck up between genial Bobby Lennox and the fiery Jimmy Johnstone (even though 'Jinky' returned to Scotland for his wedding midway through the tour). But above all, they would play together, away from the pressures of a normal season, amidst a variety of locations, atmospheres and standards of competition which would stand them in good stead for the rigours to come.

San Francisco, the venue on 2nd June for the second leg of the triple-header against Spurs, would a year later become the world capital of the 'hippie' cult of love and peace, the city of *flower power*. Even though the match was (nominally) a friendly, it is debatable whether Big Jock would have sent his players out to face the Londoners with flowers in their hair if the 'beautiful people' had emerged twelve months earlier! Certainly, no favours were being exchanged as Celtic again came out on top, this time 2-1, with goals from Lennox and Auld, while the great Dave Mackay replied for Tottenham. Three days later the mini-series came to a controversial end in Vancouver, where the rival tourists fought out a 1-1 draw. Celtic dominated the match, but with only a solitary Lennox goal to show for that supremacy, Spurs were able to snatch a face-saving equaliser five minutes from time through a disputed Terry Venables counter. Thus a highly-accomplished Tottenham side, which went on to win the F.A. Cup the following season, only narrowly avoided an embarrassing three-match whitewash by a Celtic whose self-belief was growing with every game of an inspirational tour.

Thousands of miles away, back on the home front, this blossoming self-confidence was starting to be reflected in a groundswell of optimism that the team was beginning to develop into something *special*. Celtic supporters, cruelly starved of sustained success during the fallow years of the late 'fifties (though that decade was mercifully punctuated by some of the most famous milestones in Celtic history) and early 'sixties, were desperate to acclaim modern heroes in green and white, men to compare with the legends of the great Maley era: the likes of Quinn, Napier, Gallacher, Thomson and McGrory. Post-war Celtic giants were pretty thin on the ground - probably only Peacock, Evans, Tully, Jock Stein himself (for his qualities of leadership) and perhaps Crerand and McNeill of the newer breed could stand comparison with their illustrious predecessors. Even *they* had mainly flattered to deceive, offering the fans only occasional crumbs of comfort (albeit succulent ones!), without ever delivering the regular flow of honours which Celtic followers of that former age had come to consider as their birthright. Now, as news of the unbeaten run in the Americas, continuing with a gutsy 2-2 draw against Bayern Munich of West Germany in San Francisco on Thursday,

10th June, kept filtering back through the media, the realisation of Celtic's growing stature as a real force to be reckoned with, not only domestically but also in the European arena, was hardening. Bayern were to go on to win the European Cup Winners' Cup, beating none other than Rangers 1-0 in Nuremberg the following May but they could not intimidate the East End half of the 'Old Firm'. Although the Germans forged a 2-0 lead, Celtic showed magnificent fighting spirit to overcome their opponents' physical approach and level the match with the seemingly inevitable Lennox goal, plus one from Joe McBride. According to Ken Gallacher of the Daily Record, Celtic were desperately unlucky not to go on to win.

By the time the final game of the tour came around, against Atlas of Mexico, in Los Angeles on 12th June, the playing strength of the party had been reduced to just twelve. In the course of the odyssey across the North American continent, the services had been lost of Frank McCarron, Willie O'Neill, John Cushley and Jim Brogan through injury - and Jimmy Johnstone through marriage! Despite such depletion, Atlas were duly dispatched 1-0 and Celtic ended their epic voyage of self-discovery with a formidable record:

Played 11, Won 8, Drawn 3, Lost 0, For 47, Against 6

The party returned home to enjoy a summer full of sporting interest: On 14th June, Walter McGowan of Burnbank defeated Italian, Salvatore Burruni, to capture the World Flyweight Boxing Championship; the graceful Spaniard, Manuel Santana, won the penultimate amateur Wimbledon Men's Singles title, beating Denny Ralston of the United States in the final; and Jack Nicklaus shot his way to the first of his three British Open victories at Muirfield in July, while a certain soccer tournament was taking place in England, the less said about which the better. For the record, some of the top discs of this period in the Golden Age of Pop were 'Pretty Flamingo', by Manfred Mann, the Rolling Stones' 'Paint It Black', 'Strangers In The Night', from Frank Sinatra and the inevitable Beatles chart-topper, in this case 'Paperback Writer'.

As postscript to this *American Dream Tour* and preface to a historic campaign, Celtic faced Manchester United in a pre-season friendly at Parkhead on Saturday, 6th August, 1966, just one week after England were crowned World Champions. United fielded Bobby Charlton and Nobby Stiles of the victorious national team, plus another World Cup squad member, John Connelly, who had played in the sectional games - before Alf Ramsey decided to dispense with wingers! The 'Red Devils' also boasted the incomparable George Best, who, in company with Charlton and Denis Law, formed arguably the most potent and celebrated trio of attackers ever to grace any single team in the English game. The heart of yet another man in red that day, the gifted Pat Crerand, still belonged to his first love, Celtic, whom he had only left with the most extreme reluctance in January, 1963. As the teams left the field at the end of the game, which Celtic dominated to win 4-1 (a spectacular result by any standard, and a clear indication that the 'Green Machine' was ready to fly), Jock Stein wrapped his arm around Pat's shoulder and the two disappeared up the tunnel deep in friendly conversation. With Crerand's well-known high regard for Stein, who had coached him in his early days at Celtic, eyebrows were raised. Could a shock return to the Parkhead fold possibly be on the cards? Such delicious speculation lasted only a few days - Stein had made his plans and Pat had his own destiny to pursue with United, starting with the English League Championship that very season.

Celtic, for their part, were primed and ready for their Wonder Year.

Chapter Two

Early Days: A Taste of Things to Come

Season 1966/67 began in earnest for Celtic at Tynecastle, where they played their opening League Cup sectional match against Hearts in miserable, rainy weather more suited to late November than mid August, the 13th to be exact. Hearts chose to mark the occasion by increasing admission prices to the terracing, hoping, no doubt, to cash in on Celtic's even greater-than-usual drawing power as 'born-again' Champions of Scotland. The plan backfired, however, with the bad weather and inflated costs conspiring to persuade many supporters to stay at home. The game actually drew the smallest crowd for many years to see Celtic at Tynecastle.

Those stay-at-home fans missed out on the start of a burst of goalscoring by a Celtic player such as had not been witnessed since Jimmy McGrory's heyday. Joe McBride scored both goals in Celtic's 2-0 win, then followed up with a 'hat-trick', including a penalty, in the 6-0 rout of Clyde the following midweek at Celtic Park, with Bobby Lennox (2) and Steve Chalmers also netting. The bustling centre, so reminiscent of his great predecessors in that position, grabbed four more as St Mirren were put to the sword 8-2 at Parkhead on Saturday, 20th August. Lennox and Chalmers repeated their respective midweek performances and Bertie Auld opened his account for good measure.

The following Monday, 22nd August, threw up Rangers at Ibrox in a first-round Glasgow Cup tie. Celtic's early play exemplified their blossoming confidence and the support sensed that Rangers' long-standing psychological edge had been blunted at last. Captain Billy McNeill shot Celtic ahead in the eighth minute, scoring uncharacteristically with a low left-footer under Billy Ritchie's body when the ball broke to him following a free-kick on the left-hand edge of the six-yard box. Thereafter, wee Bobby Lennox took control, making the match his own. The second goal, midway through the first half, was the goal of the season thus far. Swerving past John Greig, Bobby crashed a rising left-foot drive into Ritchie's postage-stamp corner. After the interval, Lennox went on to complete a magical personal performance with two more goals, the first coming when he sprung Rangers' offside trap, again outpacing the hapless Greig to steer the ball delicately wide of the outrushing 'keeper and in off the post. The other, *his* third and Celtic's fourth, was a low right-foot drive from eighteen yards, having himself engineered the room to shoot. A truly memorable night for Celtic, a magnificent individual triumph for the 'Buzz-Bomb' and assuredly the altered shape of things for some time to come!

In the wake of this second crushing defeat of Rangers since the turn of the year, the realisation began to dawn on the Celtic support that there simply wasn't a team in the land capable of matching the 'Bhoys' when the mood took them - and Jock Stein saw to it that the mood took them virtually every time *they* took the field! The nagging inconsistency of the early 'sixties was a thing of the past. Stein was a firm believer in the 'horses for courses' theory and he regularly switched his stable around. This was most noticeable amongst the forwards, where Lennox, Chalmers and Hughes would alternate in partnership with Joe McBride, Charlie Gallagher was a frequent deputy for Auld when the occasion required and only the incomparable Jimmy Johnstone remained a constant. How could it have been otherwise, barring unavailability? By contrast, the defence virtually picked itself, with the hitherto perennial reserve, Willie O'Neill, enjoying an extended run at left-back, Tommy Gemmell moving over to the right side of the back line to accommodate him. This permutation appeared to be a direct result of Jim Craig's unavailability for the American tour on account of his university exams in dentistry. He would face a stiff fight to regain his place.

The League Cup section was duly wrapped up with maximum points, Hearts and Clyde surrendering 3-0 at Parkhead and 3-1 at Shawfield respectively. McBride scored a brace in each of these games and was bang on course to establish some kind of record for the tournament by scoring multiples in every match, until St Mirren managed to restrict Celtic to a single-goal win at Love Street, with Bobby Murdoch doing the needful as Joe drew an uncharacteristic blank. ***This encounter was also historic in the sense that Willie O'Neill became Celtic's first-ever substitute in a competitive match.***

Interestingly, Celtic were awarded penalty kicks in four of their six sectional matches, all converted by the voracious McBride, equally bearing testimony to the team's attacking prowess and providing salutary food for thought to the eternal cynics who forever muttered darkly about Celtic 'never being given anything' by Scottish referees.

September, 1966 saw Harold Wilson firmly established in 10 Downing Street, his Labour government enjoying a comfortable overall majority of ninety-six seats in the House of Commons. Those ubiquitous Beatles were still equally firmly in control of the pop charts, their 'Yellow Submarine' (which was given a musical respray for a popular Celtic terracing ditty of the day) having torpedoed all opposition. The euphemistically-named 'Cultural Revolution' in China, inspired and led by Communist Party Chairman, Mao Tse-Tung, was just a month old, but Celtic's more benign 'Steinsurrection' was already into its eighteenth month and just getting into full swing.

The League Championship campaign began on 10th September, with a satisfying 3-0 win over Clyde at Shawfield - no mean feat at the time, for this was the Rutherglen men's strongest team for ten years and the 'Bully Wee' would end the season in third place. The following Wednesday, 14th September, brought the first leg of a potentially hazardous League Cup quarter-final against Dunfermline at Celtic Park. Despite the team's remarkable flying start to the season, the fans were well aware of the Fifers' ability to upset the applecart, especially in cup competition. However, such fears were groundless as, in the event, the tie was over as a contest almost before it had begun!

With only twenty-three minutes on the clock, Celtic were, incredibly, 5-1 ahead. Captain Billy McNeill had set the bandwagon rolling with a headed goal in only thirty seconds, John Hughes made it two in four minutes and Bertie Auld got the first of a double seven minutes later. A certain Alex Ferguson, then making a name for himself as a 'no-nonsense', bustling centre-forward, pulled one back for the 'Pars', but the whirlwind continued unabated. McBride rammed home Celtic's fourth from the penalty spot (yes, another one!) in twenty minutes and Jimmy Johnstone concluded the scoring for a first half which underlined one of the great strengths of this team, the ability to get goals regularly from so many different positions. The first *eighth* of the tie had yielded an astonishing six goals! Inevitably, the remainder of the match was a bit of an anti-climax. Ferguson and Auld grabbed another goal apiece after Hunter had scored Dunfermline's second. The final score of 6-3 flattered the Fifers, who clearly hadn't learned the lesson as far as Billy McNeill was concerned, for 'Caesar' was again allowed to open the scoring in a comfortable 3-1 canter on 21st September in the return leg at East End Park. The 9-4 aggregate was no more than Celtic deserved. They were developing an awesome ability to crush, ruthlessly, even the sternest opposition the domestic scene had to offer ... it now remained to be seen if this irresistible form could be sustained in the wider, more demanding, European arena.

Sandwiched between the two Dunfermline games was the first 'Old Firm' league match of the season, at Parkhead. Establishing a pattern that was to be repeated time and again in the early Stein years, Celtic hit Rangers with two quick goals and thereafter easily kept the Ibrox men at arm's length for the remainder of the afternoon. In the very first minute, Bertie Auld capitalised on slack marking to fire home a snap shot from just inside the box. Three minutes later, it was

Photograph courtesy of Evening Times/Herald

Joe McBride gets a close-up of Billy McNeill's early goal against Dunfermline at Celtic Park, 14th September, 1966.

effectively all over. Bobby Murdoch's attempt to blast a hole through Rangers' defensive wall from a twenty-yard free-kick resulted in the ball rebounding to his feet and this time 'Murdie' wrong-footed the entire Ibrox defence with a beautifully flighted return which sailed high past a stranded Billy Ritchie. It was a masterly shot. Like a great 'touch' tennis player frustrating a cumbersome opponent with a deftly-angled volley, or a master golfer feathering a chip holeside from an impossible lie in the rough, Murdoch's play exemplified that crucial extra dimension of speed of thought coupled with precision of execution which so characterised Celtic at that time. For the record, this was how the teams lined up that day:

CELTIC :- Simpson; Gemmell & O'Neill; Murdoch, McNeill & Clark; Johnstone, Lennox, McBride, Auld & Hughes.

RANGERS :- Ritchie; Provan & Greig; Millar, McKinnon & D. Smith; Wilson, A. Smith, Forrest, McLean & Johnston.

In an attempt to buy their way back to the top of Scottish football, Rangers had paid Aberdeen £45,000 in the close-season for their classy left-half, Dave Smith, already a Scotland internationalist. Perhaps seen as a natural successor to Jim Baxter, transferred to Sunderland a year previously, Smith, although a very fine player in his own right, lacked the self-assured arrogance and downright cheek which set 'Slim Jim' apart. Such qualities were now more prevalent at the East End of town! Alex Smith (no relation), a hard-working inside-forward, had followed from Dunfermline, also during the summer shutdown, for £55,000. This lavish outlay of £100,000 had staggered the country. At that time, such extravagance was more breathtaking than the expenditure of ten times that amount on a single player would be nowadays. Rangers' manager, Scot Symon, was a prudent, conservative man by nature. That he was prepared to spend on such a massive scale underlined the Ibrox determination to reassert their presumed natural ascendancy in Scotland at any cost. It seems it was *ever* thus.

The wins over Dunfermline and Rangers were followed by a potentially tough league visit to Dens Park. Dundee had not managed to sustain their success of the early 'sixties, when the League Championship had been won in the epic campaign of 1961/62. Through the sadly-inevitable dismantling of the backbone of the title-winning side, most notably commanding centre-half Ian Ure and prolific goalscorer Alan Gilzean, who were lured south to Arsenal and Tottenham Hotspur respectively, the 'Dark Blues' had become a depleted force - but they still represented daunting opposition, particularly on their own patch. This is borne out by the fact that Celtic had to come from behind to win, eventually, by the odd goal, 2-1, with Steve Chalmers netting the winner twelve minutes from time. Not many would run Celtic so close as the season unfolded.

And so to Europe. Celtic had been drawn against F.C. Zurich, of Switzerland, in the first round of the Champions' Cup. The first leg was played at Celtic Park on Wednesday, 28th September, 1966 and ***the following eleven players became the first to represent Celtic in Europe's premier club competition:***

Simpson; Gemmell & O'Neill; Murdoch, McNeill & Clark;
Johnstone, McBride, Chalmers, Auld & Hughes.

The Swiss fielded Ladislao Kubala (a survivor of the 'Magical Magyars', the legendary Hungarian national side of the early 'fifties) on the left wing, perhaps mindful that Tommy Gemmell had been destroyed by one of Kubala's international contemporaries, Sandor, when Jimmy McGrory's young Celtic side, containing seven of the men who would face Zurich, crumbled under pressure and lost 4-0 away to M.T.K. Budapest, having won the first leg of their European Cup-Winners' Cup semi-final 3-0 at Parkhead in season 1963/64. That agonising failure in a sometimes brutal encounter, for which those immature Celts were probably ill-equipped in terms of experience, is still recalled to this day with anguish by many Celtic supporters. Deprived of today's commonplace live television coverage, a distraught radio audience had to endure nailbiting tension as the dream of a first European final slipped away. Fortunately for Celtic, Gemmell was now older and wiser than he had been in April 1964 and the aging Kubala was a yard or two slower than Sandor had then been. ***Indeed, it was Gemmell who earned the distinction of Celtic's first ever goal in the European Cup,*** scoring with a typical raging drive from well outside the box, on the right. Such a spectacular strike befitted Celtic's début in the tournament and a solid opening victory was assured when Joe McBride added a second five minutes later to finally overcome Zurich's stubborn resistance. The match ended in unexpected controversy, however, as the referee incensed the 50,000 crowd by disallowing an apparent third goal, again from McBride, ruling that he had blown the final whistle before Joe's netbound effort had crossed the line! It is, it seems, ever Celtic's destiny to be on the wrong end of bizarre decisions.

The players, probably feeling the insecurity of their inexperience at that level, were convinced that Zurich would have a real go at them in Switzerland on 5th October. Jock Stein, however, was more sanguine, correctly assessing that they had nothing new to offer. Gemmell killed the tie in the twenty-second minute with a virtual carbon copy of his opening goal of the Glasgow leg and Chalmers unceremoniously buried it with a second before half-time. Fittingly, it was big 'T.G.' again who put the decisive finishing touch to a handsome 5-0 aggregate victory, converting a forty-eighth minute penalty (fans of the period will recall his style warmly). The spot-kick was awarded when Lennox, who had replaced McBride in the only team change from the first leg, was pulled down in the box by defender Neumann. The Scots finished the match totally in control, much to the delight of the contingent of travelling supporters in the 23,000 crowd, while the commendably sporting Swiss fans rang their cowbells in admirable appreciation of their visitors' commanding performance.

Celtic had earlier ushered in October in fine style, exhibiting their full repertoire of party tricks in a squelching 6-1 romp against St Johnstone on the first of the month. Johnstone, Lennox and McBride grabbed a brace apiece, to the grateful delight of the vast bulk of 24,000 soggy spectators, most of whom appeared to be either crammed under the cover of the new enclosure or huddled at the back of the 'Celtic End'. The second round of the European Cup was not due until the end of November, so from 5th October onwards the team could concentrate on making progress in the league and League Cup.

Following the dismissal of Zurich, Celtic faced an unbeaten Hibernian in the league at Easter Road, where Joe McBride unleashed a punishing four-goal salvo, with Steve Chalmers contributing a fifth, in a 5-3 win. It was a typically rip-roaring game in the very best tradition of the *Battles of the Greens* of that era - and already Celtic looked unstoppable. The following Saturday, 15th October, saw Airdrie, who had made an encouraging start to their season, visit Parkhead and put up spirited resistance before succumbing to goals by Lennox (2) and McBride in the second half. The 'Diamonds' were the opposition again just two days later at Hampden in the League Cup semi-final, witnessed, curiously, by 4,000 fans fewer (37,000 to 41,000) than had watched the league match. Again Airdrie's Northern Ireland internationalist 'keeper, Roddy McKenzie, was in stubborn form, holding the Celtic machine at bay until the sixty-fourth minute, in which Murdoch netted a low shot. A second strike by McBride in seventy-five minutes sealed the Lanarkshire side's inevitable fate.

Joe McBride won his first Scotland cap, having been selected with Gemmell, Clark and Johnstone to play against Wales in Cardiff on Saturday, 22nd October. With hindsight, the game, which ended 1-1, should not really have been played at all, coming as it did the day after the grotesque disaster at Aberfan, in which 116 children and 28 adults suffocated under a mass of black slurry when rain caused a pit 'bing' to shift and engulf the local primary school. Football was such a callous intrusion into national grief that tragic weekend...

...yet life goes on, even in the wake of appalling tragedy and Celtic, too, pressed ahead, doing a 5-1 demolition job on Ayr United in a rearranged league fixture at Celtic Park on the Monday. Johnstone (2), Lennox, Hughes and Gemmell were the names on the scoresheet.

With that, the stage was set for the third 'Old Firm' confrontation of the season and the most vital to date, the League Cup showdown in a Hampden final before 94,532 fevered fans. For Rangers, the stakes must have seemed particularly high. Having been soundly whipped on their own patch and then almost contemptuously dealt-with at Celtic Park, they were desperate to avoid further humiliation at the hands of their deadliest rivals. What sweeter revenge than to waltz off with the first silverware of the season and deprive their erstwhile tormentors of retaining the trophy? Little were they to know that typically 'Glasgow' late autumn afternoon - overcast, mercifully dry and with a mild breeze blowing towards the King's Park end - that such satisfaction was still some years distant as the following squads squared up for battle on 29th October, 1966:

CELTIC :- Simpson; Gemmell, & O'Neill; Murdoch, McNeill & Clark; Johnstone, Lennox, McBride, Auld & Hughes.
Substitute: Chalmers.

RANGERS :- Martin; Johansen & Provan; Greig, McKinnon & D. Smith; Henderson, Watson, McLean, A. Smith & Johnston.
Substitute: Wilson.

To help while away the nervy pre-match build-up, some inventive Rangers fans, taking mischievous advantage of the prevailing wind, were releasing balloons in taunting bunches of red, white and blue towards their opposite numbers, helplessly facing the breeze at the far end. As one particular blue balloon trundled its way upfield, it was bang on course for the gaping Celtic goal. The legions in blue collectively noticed the invading toy's unerring progress and an exultant roar of expectancy swelled as it bounced on inexorably towards the enemy net. As time seemed momentarily suspended, a young fan suddenly dashed to the rescue from the massed Celtic ranks behind the goal. Dodging past the 'Polis' who moved to intercept him, the youngster raced purposefully onto the pitch and joyously booted the offending sphere round the post for a 'corner', all to a derisory roar of mock relief from the terraced banks of green and white. Uncannily, this amusingly memorable little cameo would be mirrored in the game itself...

Tentative early sparring suggested that the now customary explosive start by Celtic might not be on the cards that day and indeed it was Rangers who began to make the running, with Celtic going on

Joe McBride's second-half strike against Airdrie, 15th October, 1966 gives 'keeper McKenzie no chance (Above).

A desperate clearance from right-back Johansen as time runs out for Rangers in the League Cup Final, 29th October, 1966 (Below).

Photograph courtesy of Evening Times/Herald.

A joyous Celtic party outside Hampden with the League Cup after the tense single-goal victory over Rangers.

the defensive, much to the chagrin of a support quite unfamiliar with such indignity. However, as so often happens in 'Old Firm' tussles, events began to turn against the tide. On the quarter-hour mark, Joe McBride chased down a searching long ball through a hesitant Rangers rearguard. Goalkeeper Norrie Martin, for so long the understudy to Billy Ritchie at Ibrox but who had recently displaced his out-of-form mentor, stopped a certain goal by blocking the centre's fierce drive with his leg. The Celtic support, perhaps sensing a 'sea-change', roared encouragement, convinced a breakthrough would come soon. It did, in the eighteenth minute. Bertie Auld gained possession on the half-way line and ambled up the left wing in his unmistakable, shuffling gait, cagily surveying his options. The outcome was a long, hanging cross to the back post, where McBride had lost his markers and ghosted through the inside-right channel. Joe nodded the ball down perfectly into the path of an inrushing Bobby Lennox, whose first-time volley fairly raged past the helpless Martin. It was a glorious goal and could so easily have been the pebble which would start the avalanche - but Celtic would not impose their will so readily on Rangers this time.

In fact, Ronnie Simpson was the busier 'keeper throughout. Rangers thought they had equalised in the thirty-first minute, when inside-forward Bobby Watson drove home a shot from twenty yards after Simpson's attempt at a punched clearance of a John Greig free kick landed at his feet. However, referee Tom 'Tiny' Wharton came to Celtic's rescue, ruling that the veteran goalie had been impeded. On such incidents matches can turn, titles and cups can be won and lost. Perhaps the ability to make such decisions under pressure and in the full glare of publicity is what sets referees out as a breed apart. Certainly, Wharton was a giant amongst the whistlers of the day, in more ways than one.

The first half ended with Celtic grimly hanging on to their slender, fragile lead. Hopes that the resumption would bring a change in the pattern were soon dashed as Rangers began the second half with renewed zeal. Time and again they swept forward menacingly, only to falter in front of goal. ***In the sixty-fifth minute, Steve Chalmers made history by becoming the first substitute to be used in a cup final - ANY cup final - in Scotland*** when he replaced the enigmatic and on the day, ineffective, John Hughes. In the 1965 final, Hughes had been rampant, unstoppable, as he raced past Rangers' Danish full-back, Kai Johansen, at will and he had repeated that medicine in the 5-1 league rout at Parkhead on 3rd January. This time, though, 'Yogi' was having one of his off-days, when he would look totally hapless.

The introduction of Chalmers made absolutely no difference to the flow of the game and Tommy McLean missed a snip, blazing over the bar when Willie Johnston had laid a perfect pass into his path, right on the six-yard line. Then followed *The Great Escape*, which had been inadvertantly 'trailed' in the pre-match run-up. With only fifteen minutes remaining and just three after McLean's glaring miss, a Greig through ball found Alex Smith racing clear with only Simpson to beat. As he bore down on the advancing 'keeper, Smith stumbled, only managing to prod the ball weakly towards the empty net. Attackers and defenders alike froze, seemingly mesmerised as the ball trickled goalwards. It seemed no-one would react. Then Willie O'Neill, so often the unsung hero, snapped out of the trance and set off in pursuit, clearing the ball right off the line, just as the heroic young fan had done earlier with the incoming balloon. It was a case of mass *déja-vu* as the Celtic support heaved a collective sigh of relief.

The match seemed to just peter out after that, with Rangers continuing to throw everything into attacks of increasing desperation as Celtic resolutely held the line. Jock Stein's summing up was terse and concise: 'We did not play as well as we can. We have often played better against Rangers and lost. We did just enough to win this one.'

One down, then - and more to come than anyone would have dared hope at that point in time!

On 2nd November, Celtic took on Stirling Albion in a re-scheduled home league fixture. By the third minute of the second half, they led 7-1. McBride had notched up yet another 'hat-trick', Chalmers a brace, Johnstone and Auld one each. Understandably, the foot came off the gas a bit and Albion cashed in to the tune of two more consolation goals. There can be no doubt, however, that Celtic could easily have gone on into double figures. They were by then getting to be so far ahead of even their strongest challengers that the situation was verging on the farcical. They had demonstrated that they could drop down several gears and still see off a super-motivated Rangers in a cup final situation. Who in Scotland could possibly stop them?

Just as such unhealthy speculation was beginning to set in and it was starting to be suggested that the team might be capable of going through the entire league campaign without dropping a point, St Mirren came to Parkhead on Guy Fawkes Day and lit a rocket under Celtic. With McNeill out injured and Gemmell at centre-half, Jim Craig was recalled at right-back with Hampden hero, Willie O'Neill, moving to the left. St Mirren goalkeeper and future Celt, Denis Connaghan, had an outstanding match and Celtic were strangely uneasy throughout. Although Gemmell put Celtic ahead just after the interval, it came as no real surprise when 'Saints' equalised seven minutes later. Bobby Murdoch, of all people, got himself sent off - Celtic's first and only dismissal of the season. Yes, it was *one of those games*. In the end, the fans were just grateful that the team had maintained its unbeaten record. Hopefully, this minor setback would jolt them out of any possible complacency. Incidentally, playing (at left-back) for St Mirren that day was a youngster destined, in due course, not only to win a European Cup winner's medal of his own but also to score one of the most memorable goals in World Cup history. But Argentina was still a dozen years into the future for Archie Gemmill!

Celtic quickly shook off the disappointment of dropping their first league point to beat Falkirk 3-0 at Brockville, with McBride scoring twice (1 pen.) and Auld getting the other. On Wednesday, 16th November, the club provided six players for Scotland's 2-1 victory over Northern Ireland in the Home International Championship. Bobby Lennox made his international début in that match and was joined by Gemmell, Clark, Murdoch, Chalmers and McBride. Wee Bobby fully justified his selection with a début goal and just for good measure, Bobby Murdoch got the other to underline Celtic's contribution. Around this era, there was a strong lobby advocating the selection of the entire Celtic team to represent Scotland at international level. It is easy to understand why, but for whatever reason, it never actually happened. Perhaps it is just as well.....

On 19th November, an unforgettable league match was staged at East End Park. Three times Celtic trailed Dunfermline by two goals. After a goalless first thirty minutes, the dam burst. International winger Hugh Robertson put the 'Pars' one up just after the half-hour mark and ex-Motherwell man Pat Delaney, son of Celtic legend Jimmy, added another just two minutes later. Bobby Murdoch pegged one back in double-quick time before Bert Paton restored the Fifers' two-goal advantage with the fourth goal of an explosive eight minute spell. Jimmy Johnstone kept the pot boiling and brought Celtic right back into it by half-time with their second goal two minutes from the break, only for that man Alex Ferguson to blunt the fightback by banging in a fourth Dunfermline counter with the second half barely three minutes old. Celtic's response was to keep plugging away, remorselessly building up irresistible pressure on the Dunfermline defence until Auld reduced the deficit to one again in the sixty-second minute. Goal-machine Joe McBride then induced near-delirium in the travelling support when he squared things at 4-4 with twenty-one minutes remaining. Thereafter, the match became a nerve-jangling, ding-dong battle, as both teams chased a decisive fifth goal. When it inevitably came, it was via the penalty spot, in the final minute of play and it fell to McBride to close out a truly breathtaking clash which was arguably the domestic game of the season. The cavalier Stein philosophy of playing to the final whistle and aiming simply to outscore the opposition, irrespective of goals conceded, was perhaps never more graphically or dramatically illustrated.

Joe scored with another last-minute penalty the following week, 26th November, against Hearts at Celtic Park, the closing goal of a comprehensive 3-0 victory and his own second of the game. The opener had been a spectacularly-volleyed own-goal by the 'Jam Tarts' luckless skipper, George Miller.

Meanwhile, Celtic had been drawn to play French Champions, Nantes, in the second round of the Champions' Cup, with the first leg away from home on Wednesday, 30th November. Having fallen behind to a goal by Magny just after the quarter hour mark, they drew level through McBride in the twenty-fourth minute. Stein's stormtroopers fully lived up to the manager's pre-match promise to attack and actually stepped up the pace in the second half. The payback came in the form of further goals by Lennox (50 mins) and Chalmers (67 mins) which underpinned a highly creditable result in front of a strangely subdued and undemonstrative home crowd, who had clearly not expected such a bullish approach from their comparatively unknown visitors. So far, so good...

Chapter Three

Good Buy, Big Man - Goodbye, Joe!

Outwith the odd spectacular gaff, reminding us he was really only human after all, Jock Stein was one of the shrewdest operators the Scottish transfer market has seen. No single piece of business underlined that expertise more emphatically than the happy acquisition of 'Wispy' Willie Wallace from Hearts on 6th December, 1966. Several factors had influenced the manager's decision to go for the chunky forward in what would prove to rank amongst the club's most significant signings ever: firstly, centre-forward Joe McBride was struggling with a cartilage problem which might require surgery at any time - experienced cover was thin on the ground; secondly, Wallace was in dispute with the Edinburgh club, a problem inherited by manager John Harvey from his predecessor, Tommy Walker and the new man's apparent sympathy with the player's position had led him to promise not to stand in his way if a suitable move came along; and thirdly, Rangers were known to be interested. If Stein could edge *them* out, he would strike a major psychological blow in the constant battle for domestic supremacy and silverware.

The story of this masterly signing would have graced a John Le Carré plot. Following the goalless draw with Kilmarnock at Rugby Park on 3rd December (only the second league point dropped and the first competitive match of the season in which they had failed to score), newspapers reported that Celtic were poised to bid £60,000 for Coventry City's Scottish forward, Ian Gibson. Having already been linked with Wallace, the Gibson rumour (it may well have been no *more* than that) let Hearts know that Celtic had other options.

Perhaps, though, the most crucial factors were circumstance and timing. Celtic were installed at Seamill, preparing for the second leg of the Nantes tie at Parkhead a few days later. Meanwhile Rangers, their potential rivals for Wallace's signature, were conveniently out of the country. They were in West Germany, successfully defending a 2-0 first-leg lead established at Ibrox, to eliminate the holders, Borussia Dortmund, from the European Cup Winners' Cup, en route to their very own Nuremberg trial. Stein struck in the domestic vacuum, snapping up Wallace for a bargain £27,000 - an absolute steal for a proven prolific goalscorer who was versatile, two-footed, experienced and a current internationalist. Willie had played for Scotland against England at Hampden seven months previously and would do so again in the glorious Wembley dethronement of 'Ramsey's Robots' the following May.

At the time, the British record transfer had been frozen since December 1962 at the £115,000 paid to Torino by Manchester United to end the Italian exile of Denis Law. Six-figure fees were practically unheard-of (as was the current buzz-word 'inflation') in those simpler days of relative economic stability, spanning the period from the end of Harold 'Supermac' Macmillan's 'You've never had it so good' era to Harold 'Gannex' Wilson's 'Pound in your pocket' devaluation of 1967. The only time Law's ransome was ever threatened was when Everton and Leeds United engaged in a rather unseemly and unprecedented public auction over England's World Cup workhorse, Alan Ball, of Blackpool, in the glutinous euphoria of the immediate aftermath of the 1966 Finals. The pint-sized, red-haired hustler finally plumped for Everton, by which time the bidding had soared to an astonishing £110,000. It would be a further two years before the record was broken.

The breach finally came when Southampton manager Ted Bates quoted Spurs £125,000 for towering centre-forward, Martin Chivers and was astounded that Tottenham boss Bill Nicholson agreed to pay. Bates, hoping to retain his powerful striker, had been confident his astronomical demand would deter even the most determined bidder. In the event, the Chivers deal opened the transfer floodgates - within months Alan Clarke moved from Fulham to Leicester City for the earth-shattering sum of £150,000, even though, in common with Chivers (but unlike Wallace), 'Sniffer', as Clarke would come to be known in his glory days with Leeds United and England, was not yet an internationalist. In fairness, both Chivers and Clarke were to go on to justify their massive valuations but other less and less gifted players began to switch clubs with bewildering regularity and for ever-increasing sums of money. By those standards, indexed to today's values, Stein's acquisition of Wallace was like plundering a £4,000,000 player for around £750,000 - certainly one of the slickest pieces of British transfer business ever.

Ironically, as it turned out, Jock probably need not have worried about the Ibrox factor. Wallace later went on record that, aware as he was of Rangers' interest, he knew he stood a far better chance of collecting domestic - and possibly European - honours with Celtic at that time and would almost certainly have opted for them, anyway, given a straight choice.

Of course, under the prevailing rules, Willie would not be eligible for European Cup duty until the semi-final, should Celtic progress that far. He must have been impressed, however, by the manner in which his new team-mates cruised into the quarter-finals at the expense of Nantes on only the second day of his new job. The side which ran out comfortable 3-1 victors at Celtic Park on Wednesday, 7th December was:

Simpson; Gemmell & O'Neill; Murdoch, McNeill & Clark;
Johnstone, Gallagher, Chalmers, Auld & Lennox.

Photograph courtesy of Evening Times/Herald

A little cameo of Jimmy Johnstone's sparkling display in the European Cup second round, second leg against Nantes, Celtic Park, 7th December 1966.

Johnstone gave Celtic a thirteenth minute lead and although Georgen equalised for the Frenchmen nine minutes from half-time, it didn't spoil the party too much as 'Jinky' turned on his unique brand of wizardry in the second half, laying on simple scores for Chalmers and Lennox to underpin an emphatic 6-2 aggregate.

The new Celt duly made his début in the home match against Motherwell the following Saturday. Steve Chalmers it was, though, who took the scoring honours, upstaging Wallace and everybody else by rattling Celtic 2-0 up at half-time and clinching his 'hat-trick' seven minutes from the end, thereby apparently putting the issue beyond doubt after George Murray had re-kindled the 'Steelmen's' hopes with a goal five minutes earlier. No sooner was the back-slapping over, however, than Ronnie Simpson was again picking the ball out of the back of his net, where it had been planted by Motherwell's Lindsay. Nervous fears of an imminent upset were soon quelled by Bobby Murdoch restoring Celtic's two-goal advantage a few moments later to conclude a quickfire four-goal exchange inside ten see-saw minutes. The 4-2 scoreline was not at all untypical of a more free-scoring football era - *particularly when Celtic were involved.* The heat of a thrilling match saw Motherwell's young centre-forward sent off. It was his first appearance against Celtic and he was destined to become a notorious 'bad boy' of Scottish soccer in his five-and-a-half seasons at Fir Park. The unenviable reputation did nothing to deter his future career progression, however. His name? John 'Dixie' Deans!

Having played himself in quietly, 'Wispy' opened his personal account a week later against Partick Thistle in the league at Celtic Park. It was a simple enough affair, almost routine, hardly the dream start he might have wished for. Only two minutes had elapsed on a dull, grey afternoon, when Willie popped up on the Thistle line to nod home after Joe McBride had headed a free-kick back across goal. Stevie Chalmers had added a second in the fourteenth minute before Wallace *really* endeared himself to the Celtic support with an explosive counter ten minutes later. Celtic were shooting towards the 'Rangers End' and from the 'Jungle', just on the half-way line, the great man was clearly heard to bark, 'Leave it!' as the ball was ballooned into the air by the Thistle defence following a Celtic corner. Wallace, taking responsibility for his sharp command, hit the ball on the drop from fully twenty yards, a glorious half-volley which fairly screamed high into the net. Now *that* was more like the thing! Bobby Murdoch made it 4-0 in thirty-two minutes and it was clear that the Stein goal machine was in overdrive. A youthful Arthur Duncan, later to star in the fine Hibs side of the early 'seventies and to play for Scotland, pegged one back for Thistle with a smart goal in thirty-six minutes to establish a half-time scoreline of 4-1. After the break, Joe McBride reminded us all that *he* was still around (though, sadly, not for much longer), making it 5-1 in fifty-six minutes. Tommy Gibb, Thistle's elegant half-back, pulled another goal back for the 'Jags' shortly after the hour mark, but Chalmers restored the four-goal cushion with his own second and Celtic's sixth, ten minutes later.There was a strong Celtic connection in the Thistle ranks that day in the persons of former Parkhead favourite John Divers at centre and Jock Stein's future assistant, Davie McParland, at inside-right.

The Saturday before Christmas is traditionally the worst of the season attendance-wise. Such was the attraction of the 1966 Celts, though, that Pittodrie Park, Aberdeen, held a respectably large crowd of 31,000 for their visit on Christmas Eve. The 'Dons' were as tough a nut to crack on their own patch then as they are now, so it was with some relief that Celtic left the 'Granite City' with their unbeaten record still intact. Lennox had put Celtic ahead after twenty-five minutes but Harry Melrose, their old adversary from the 1961 and 1965 Cup Finals against Dunfermline, levelled for Aberdeen on the half-hour mark. Celtic may have gained - or, as Jock Stein would have it, *lost* a point - but worst of all, this was the match that finally brought down the curtain on Joe McBride's season.

One of the most outstanding statistics of Celtic's remarkable 'Season in the Sun' remains that its wondrous feats were achieved despite being deprived of such a prolific scorer for so long. History records that McBride had run up an astonishing thirty-seven goals before Christmas and we can only speculate as to what his tally for the season might have ended up had cruel fate not intervened. As it was, he remained the country's joint-top-scorer at the season's end without kicking a ball in anger for almost the final five months. That truly remarkable fact and the style, courage and personality which underlie it, to a great extent explain the genuine warmth and affection with which Joe is remembered and why, in Celtic circles, he is almost universally considered the twelfth 'Lisbon Lion'.

Joe was injured in a tackle in the first half and had to be replaced. Tragically, the knee trouble which had threatened for several weeks and expedited the purchase of Wallace, could be contained no longer. The consistent goalscoring which had epitomised the McBride career had not been without cost. The inevitable wear and tear had brought on an agonising condition, with 'floating' pieces of bone from a flaking kneecap. This latest tackle had simply brought matters to a head. An operation was now urgently required and in those days before 'keyhole' surgery and laser technology, that meant, at best, a lengthy lay-off. Joe *would* return, but things were never the same again.

It was some comfort under such circumstances that, on the league front, things didn't look too bad, as Rangers, the only realistic challengers for the title, were four points adrift. Before the year was out, though, that lead would be halved, as Celtic finally lost a competitive match, going down 3-2 to Dundee United at Tannadice on Hogmanay, despite leading 1-0 and 2-1. Finn Dossing, one of United manager Jerry Kerr's mid-sixties Scandinavian imports, equalised Bobby Lennox's twelfth minute opener but Willie Wallace immediately responded to restore Celtic's lead and so it remained until eighteen minutes from time. Then the roof fell in, as late goals from United veteran Dennis Gillespie and inside-forward Graham Mitchell, in the seventy-second and seventy-fifth minutes, blew the league race wide open. Suddenly, the awful prospect of a January slump, such as had almost cost Celtic the Championship the previous season, reared its ugly head and anxiety took root amongst the support.

The team was due to face Rangers at Ibrox on Monday, 2nd January. A home win would revitalise the challengers, hoisting Rangers level at the top on points and ahead on *goal average,* the Govan men having conceded fewer goals. Then the weather intervened. Ibrox was deemed unplayable and the 'Old Firm' clash postponed. To the superstitious, this was, historically speaking, a real break for Celtic, since they had not beaten Rangers at Ibrox in the traditional Ne'erday fixture since the 'twenties.

Curiously enough, fans heading in vain for Ibrox were able to divert to Hampden and take in the last-ever South Glasgow derby between Third Lanark and Queen's Park. Thirds had long been in the death throes of alleged financial mis-management and would finally slip under in May, leaving Cathkin Park, reputedly one of the finest playing surfaces in Scotland, a ghostly museum of haunting football memories. Not so very long before, crowds had flocked to Cathcart Road to watch the 'Hi-Hi' greats - Jimmy Brownlie, Jimmy Mason and none other than Ronnie Simpson (in the 'forties). Not forgetting the last *great* Thirds team of the late 'fifties/early 'sixties, featuring such characters as wee Jocky Robertson in goal, 'Junior' McGillivray at right-back and the devastating inside-forward trio of Hilley, Harley and Gray, which helped run up 100 league goals in season 1960/61. Alas, it was a sad irony that, just as Celtic were poised to scale the pinnacle of greatness, one of their oldest and best-loved adversaries teetered on the brink of imminent oblivion. Just for the record, Thirds beat Queen's 2-0 that fateful day on a hard, but definitely playable

Hampden surface, only a few tantalising miles from the frost-bound Ibrox!

By the resumption of play for 1967, Celtic were back on song. Another shuffle of the pack saw the introduction of Craig, now freed of his prolonged academic commitments, for O'Neill, Johnstone for Hughes and Gallagher for Auld, plus the switching of Chalmers into the middle. Celtic were well and truly refreshed and raring to go again. The first league match of the year against Dundee at Parkhead on 7th January was won comfortably, 5-1. Celtic were four up inside half an hour, having led 2-0 after only five minutes play, to effectively banish any lingering fears of slump. Dundee's Wilson had the misfortune to set the bandwagon rolling with an own-goal in four minutes and Willie Wallace put the game virtually beyond the visitors one minute later. Jimmy Johnstone celebrated his first outing for a month with the third goal in twenty-one minutes and Charlie Gallagher followed suit with the best goal of the game seven minutes later. Taking a Murdoch pass with his back to goal, twelve yards out, he wheeled smartly to crack the ball high past John Arrol in the Dundee goal. Though Kenny Cameron salvaged some Tayside pride with a consolation strike six minutes into the second half, Wallace underlined Celtic's vast superiority with his own second two minutes from time.

The same line-up produced the same 5-1 scoreline the following Wednesday night against Clyde in the league at Celtic Park, although this time Celtic left it late. Chalmers scored the usual early counter in twelve minutes, but Clyde were made of stern stuff in 1967 and Joe Gilroy equalised after thirty-two minutes. It wasn't until nine minutes after the interval that Charlie Gallagher restored Celtic's advantage, but a devastating late burst of three goals in four minutes sunk the 'Bully Wee' without trace, Chalmers again, Gemmell and Lennox doing the conclusive damage.

The potential crisis (real or illusory) had apparently been averted, with the team reproducing its heady early-season form. Confirmation of the stabilisation came at Muirton Park, Perth, on Saturday, 14th January. Outwith 'Old Firm' encounters, St Johnstone away would then rank alongside Hibs at Easter Road, Hearts at Tynecastle, or Dunfermline at East End Park as one of the most difficult fixtures on the Scottish card. Yet, for the third league game in a row, Celtic won by a four-goal margin, all the goals this time coming in the second half. Johnstone bagged a brace in sixty-three and sixty-nine minutes, then Chalmers and Lennox put the icing on the cake with a goal apiece inside the closing five minutes. The good work continued at Celtic Park the following Saturday as Hibs were seen off 2-0, with Wallace opening the scoring via a strong contender for *Goal of the Season*. Picking up a pass way out on the right at the half-way line, 'Wispy' set off hell-for-leather towards the Hibs goal, outstripped the entire defence, cut into the box and unleashed a venomous drive high past a bemused Thomson Allan. Twelve minutes on the clock and another rout in prospect! This time, however, it was not to be and the Celts were restricted to just one more goal, scored by Stevie Chalmers in thirty-eight minutes. The players seemed to acquiesce in the more modest scoreline, happy to conserve their energy for the first round of the Scottish Cup the following week. Anything could happen at the stage when the minnows take on the sharks, as subsequent events would soon prove!

Saturday, 28th January, 1967, dawned unseasonably mild, a grey 'Glasgow' day with no threat of rain, but equally no promise of sun . As always, the last Saturday in January was the day the 'big guns' entered the Scottish Cup. The draw had been kind to the 'Old Firm', giving Celtic a routine-looking home tie against an industrious Arbroath side from the middle reaches of the Second Division and the men of Govan a pleasant day-trip down to the Tweed to dispatch the 'Wee Rangers' with their customary finesse. However, Berwick, inspired by their goalkeeper-coach, one Jock Wallace, had forgotten to read the script - but that's another story!

Arbroath were out of the cup before they knew what hit them, Murdoch, Gemmell and Chalmers sealing the fate of the 'Red Lichties' in not much over half an hour. By the time Bertie Auld had made it 4-0 in the eightieth minute, one of the greatest sensations ever in Scottish football history had taken place ... in England! Due to the lack of adequate floodlighting at Berwick's Shielfield Park, the cup-tie against Rangers kicked off at 2.30 p.m. instead of the normal three o'clock. This no doubt pleased the locals, who remembered the destruction visited upon them by an unruly section of the Ibrox support on the occasion of their last visit on cup business, some seven years previously. The sooner the marauding hordes from the north were off the premises, the sooner normal life could resume ... but the footballing gods had decided to suspend normal life for the time being and so it was that, even before Bobby Murdoch had opened the scoring at Parkhead, Sammy Reid had done likewise for Berwick Rangers, to give his team an unlikely thirty-fifth minute lead. Use of the 'tranny' was not so widespread in 1967 as it is now, so much of the Parkhead crowd remained blissfully ignorant and totally unsuspecting of events unfolding in the south. However, midway through the second half at Celtic Park, came an astonishing example of the 'bush telegraph' in action. It began as a sudden buzz of excitement in the main stand, which spread quickly to the 'Rangers End', thence to the 'Jungle' and finally to the 'Celtic End'. The initial tremor had by then swelled to something akin to a feeding frenzy and the whole ground seemed to bubble over as scarves and bunnets exploded into the air, while sporadic, joyous dancing broke out all over the terracing. The unlikely explanation of this rash of jubilation finally penetrated the farthest outposts, where a young lad was heard to blurt out the unimaginable: 'The Rangers've got beat 1-0 at Berwick!'

As this profound truth began to sink in, initial disbelief flowered into the familiar pogo-hugging hysteria generally reserved for a vital Celtic goal - not entirely through collective gloating at Rangers' cataclysmic misfortune (though it would be churlish to deny that *this* was the prime motive), but partially in the stark relief of the unexpected removal at the first hurdle of *the* major obstacle to Celtic's progress in the Scottish Cup. As an example of word-of-mouth communication, it was a classic. It was Athens to Marathon and Paul Revere's Ride all rolled into one. This was one occasion when the *Chinese Whispers* very definitely got it right!

Chapter Four

A Tight Squeak in The Balkans.

Over and above its profound psychological effect, Rangers' *Bungle in the Borders* had levelled out the humps considerably on the road to Hampden. With all due respect to Aberdeen, Dundee United, Hearts, Hibs and co., the shock Ibrox demise had sharpened the focus on Celtic's cup prospects. Now, given reasonable luck in the draw and a positive attitude, the men in green could anticipate a fairly comfortable run without constantly looking over their shoulders in the direction of Govan. Stein's priority now was to ensure that there would be no slacking in the league.

A healthy crowd of 23,000 crammed into Broomfield the following Saturday to watch the Celtic bandwagon flatten an Airdrie side which had lost much of its early-season zeal and was now relying on stuffy defence. Goals from Johnstone, Chalmers and Auld blew apart their precarious policy of containment. Wee Jimmy, restored to the right-wing beat after missing the Arbroath cup-tie, had returned in his scoring boots, which were on parade again at Somerset Park in the next league game on 11th February. Ayr United held out stoutly for forty minutes, but the exuberance of Celtic's play was uncontainable. 'Jinky' grabbed the opener before half-time, then a familiar scoring burst of three in five second-half minutes killed the game. Chalmers struck in the fifty-seventh and sixty-second minutes, with a John Hughes goal in between providing the filling for the tasty sandwich. 'Di Steviano' completed his 'hat-trick' late in the game to round off another breathtaking five-goal display.

The Scottish Cup draw continued to favour Celtic, pairing them with Highland Leaguers, Elgin City, at Celtic Park in the second round. Elgin were Highland League Champions, but the 'Cocks o' the North' were expected to be 'sitting ducks' at Parkhead. A huge cavalcade of supporters made the long trip south for the game, endearing themselves to the home fans by their jovial good humour and unswerving determination to enjoy their big day out, whatever the outcome. Bedecked in huge black and white top-hats, rosettes and scarves, they were, in the very best tradition, 'up for the cup'; and in the first half at

Celtic Park on 18th February, little Elgin showed absolutely no signs of being 'out for the count'. In fact, they came within two minutes of registering a half-time scoreline that would have had crowds throughout Scotland choking on their pies and Bovril as they surveyed the primitive, letter-coded scoreboards (an early marketing ploy aimed at the promotion of programme sales), which were so much a feature of football up to and throughout the 'sixties. The Highlanders held Celtic at bay for all of forty-three minutes before unaccountably caving in. Quite suddenly, a goal by Chalmers and a rapid-fire brace by Lennox gave the midway score a misleadingly predictable look. The belated caning continued in the second half, with John Hughes scoring just after the hour mark, Lennox completing his 'hat-trick' and Willie Wallace notching his first double of the campaign in the last ten minutes. What started out as a somewhat chastening experience for Celtic had thankfully ended in the sort of widely-foretold 7-0 canter which wouldn't even raise an eyebrow amongst the unwitting tea-time score-checkers.

Yet another away league fixture followed on Saturday, 25th February, the third in a curious run of four. This time Celtic were controversially held 1-1 by Stirling Albion at Annfield. Albion, then managed by former Rangers favourite Sammy Baird (and typically of that period, wearing orange 'change' jerseys apparently reserved for Celtic), made it clear from the off that they would be taking no prisoners. The match was played in a downpour, and the heavy pitch clearly favoured the home side, blunting as it did the more refined skills of their visitors. Albion took the lead after twenty-three minutes' play through a goal by right-winger Peebles and retained the advantage until half-time, despite strenuous Celtic efforts to equalise. With the trip to Yugoslavia for the European Cup quarter-final against Vojvodina looming in midweek, the last thing Celtic needed was a bitter, snarling encounter with a less-gifted bunch of desperate glory-hunters. Nagging memories of the previous February, exactly a year and a day earlier, were still fresh. Then, a shock 1-0 defeat at Annfield had violently rocked Celtic's Championship boat. Jock Stein was determined there would be no repeat and that the ship would this year stay firmly on course. The tension was relieved in fifty-two minutes, when Hughes, who, despite his height was certainly not noted for aerial expertise, headed a smart equaliser from Auld's cross. Thereafter, the game degenerated into a running battle, until, inevitably, the referee was forced into a dismissal, the early bather being Albion's brawny centre-half, Rogerson, sent packing for a bad foul on Chalmers. Celtic appeared to have weathered the storm to snatch a winner five minutes from the end, when Billy McNeill powerfully headed home a Hughes corner - but the referee had spotted some infringement not immediately obvious to anyone else, so Celtic had to be content with sound limbs and the one point.

So, bloodied but unbowed, Celtic headed for Novi Sad, in the province of Vojvodina in northern Yugoslavia. Confidence was high. As probably more than one fan put it: 'Novi Sad? They'll be *awfy* sad by the time we've finished wi' them!' Prophetic words, perhaps - but the outcome was like a golfer's scorecard, where the numbers don't even begin to tell the story. This would be a prophecy fulfilled in ecstatic agony on a torrid night of wild emotion and high drama.

Meanwhile, a remarkable Beatles run of eleven consecutive Number Ones was brought to an end by heart-throb Englebert Humperdinck, whose rather turgid ballad, 'Please Release Me', persisted at the top of the charts for five weeks, stubbornly keeping the 'Fab Four's' classic double 'A' side, 'Strawberry Fields Forever/Penny Lane' (originally intended for inclusion on the forthcoming epic 'Sergeant Pepper' album), at bay. Astonishingly, it was the first time since 'Please, Please Me', in January, 1963, that a Beatles single had failed to reach the top spot!

A 'little local difficulty' having arisen with Arab dissidents in Aden, the unenviable task of its suppression fell to the men of The Argyll & Sutherland Highlanders, under the sometimes unconventional command of the larger-than-life Lieutenant-Colonel Colin 'Mad Mitch' Mitchell.

Over in the Balkans, Celtic's first-leg objective was to do as effective a job of containment on the widely underestimated Yugoslav Champions. Actually, it had come as something of a surprise to most Celtic supporters to be playing the 'Slavs at all. The draw had paired Celtic with the winners of the Vojvodina/Atletico Madrid second round tie, which had been drawn on aggregate, going to a play-off in the Spanish capital on the toss of a coin for home advantage. Atletico had been firm favourites to go through, but Vojvodina were made of stern stuff and shocked the confident Spaniards 3-2.

Considering Celtic had never beaten a Spanish team in European competition, perhaps the upset was a good omen. On the other hand, in preparation for the quarter-final, Celtic had arranged a friendly against Yugoslav opposition, Dynamo Zagreb, in which Jock Stein, ever-alert to the need to catch the public imagination, had promised the fans a revolutionary new attacking formation. It seemed as if the idea was to reverse defensive and forward roles as Celtic lined up at Parkhead on 8th February like something of a dog's breakfast, with players out of position all over the place. John Hughes wore the No 5, while Tommy Gemmell started at outside-left (nothing too unusual in that, you might say!) but the anticipated blitz never materialised. The predicted fireworks proved to be damp squibs as Celtic, looking uncomfortably lop-sided, struggled to adjust to their strange experimental roles and the 'Slavs had the impertinence to nick a last-minute winner through inside-left Zambata, who found himself unmarked in front of the exposed Ronnie Simpson, able unchallenged to convert a low cross from the right wing for the only goal of a game which was a major disappointment to an expectant support. For once Stein's sense of theatre had let him down, as his grand East End production turned into a farce - and it was himself and Celtic who were caught with their trousers down!

When the serious business started on St David's day, 1st March, in Novi Sad, Celtic were managing to frustrate a bustling home side, surviving several close calls in the first half and appearing about to successfully ride out a mounting storm in the second period until Gemmell carelessly misdirected a pass-back. Even the normally ubiquitous John Clark could not retrieve his team-mate's rashness and prevent left-winger Stanic accepting the gift. 1-0 Vojvodina! Rejuvenated by this fortuitous breakthrough, the 'Slavs piled on the pressure with renewed vigour for the remainder of the game but Celtic held on without further loss to survive the most dangerous hurdle of the historic campaign. Although the Scottish Champions were deprived of the ineligible Wallace and the injured McBride, Vojvodina could justifiably claim to have been even more disadvantaged by the lack of a clutch of recognised first-team men for one reason or another. Three of the players who had figured in the play-off win over Atletico had to miss the first leg match against Celtic. Forwards Trivic and Pusibric had been sent off in Madrid and were suspended. Takac, another forward, who had scored the winning goal in Spain, had since been transferred to Rennes of France. A fourth vital cog in the Yugoslav machine, half-back Zemko, had not been properly registered in time to beat the three-month deadline for European eligibility. This was no less than a piece of gross administrative carelessness by Vojvodina, as the player had actually been signed in good time for registration. By comparison, Willie Wallace's signing date excluded him from quarter-final participation by a hairsbreadth. Fate, then, and human frailty had conspired to undermine Celtic's sternest European adversaries, a status the Yugoslav Champions would underline in an epic return leg in Glasgow.

Celtic's Championship defence showed no sign of faltering, despite their ongoing European exertions. They retained a two-point lead over Rangers, who, it should not be forgotten, were performing heroics of their own in the European arena. Having dismissed holders Borussia Dortmund from the Cup-Winners' Cup in the second round, they would proceed to the semi-final stage by dint of surviving the quarter-final against Real Zaragoza in Spain on 22nd March on the toss of a coin, Real having reversed Rangers' 2-0 victory at Ibrox earlier in the month. It was a curious anomaly of the time that there should be such a divergence in rules between the two principal European competitions: play-offs in the Champions' Cup, *toss-ups* in the supporting tournament!

With just ten league games remaining and only four days short of their biggest test of the season so far, the Vojvodina return, Celtic travelled to Paisley to face St Mirren on Saturday, 4th March, a bleak day of unremitting rain, which produced another gluepot of a pitch. With the strength-sapping conditions and mindful of the vital midweek fixture, Stein left Johnstone out of the starting line-up, though keeping him on the bench, while resting Chalmers completely. Big 'Yogi' filled the right wing berth, producing one of his inimitable displays of power play. Celtic led at half-time through a Wallace goal and Bobby Lennox virtually settled the outcome with a fast strike at the start of the second half. The 'Bear' scored a typical third goal, waltzing through the glaur with defenders sprawling in his wake before rounding Denis Connaghan and tapping into the empty net. Great entertainment and huge compensation for the loyal thousands braving the elements huddled under the Love Street covered enclosure! Gemmell, with a penalty and Wallace, with his own second, took the tally to five and put a high gloss on a fine win. Next stop, Seamill!

The heavy rain persisted right through to the day of the Vojvodina game and in the interests of playing conditions, Jock Stein felt obliged to request that the Yugoslavs forego the customary opportunity to train on the match pitch on the Tuesday night. This did not please his opposite number, Vujadin Boskov, one little bit, as he was naturally anxious to familiarise his players with the playing surface and perhaps more importantly, to alert them to the vastness of the Parkhead arena. For many of them, Celtic Park would be the grandest stage on which they had ever been asked to perform and the 70,000 sell-out crowd the biggest of their career to date. Though Boskov might reasonably have suspected it, this was no piece of gamesmanship and Stein stood his ground resolutely, expressly forbidding training at the stadium itself but cordially offering the 'Slavs full access to the Barrowfield facility.

With the continuing ineligibility of Wallace and the enforced absence of McBride, Stein assessed his attacking options and gambled on omitting Bertie Auld from the team, the jersey being handed to his perennial understudy for the inside-left berth, Charlie Gallagher, on account of Gallagher's dead-ball expertise and his penchant for striking long, accurate passes to running forwards. With the pace of Chalmers and Lennox providing the main forward threat, Jock considered Charlie's pinpoint skill to be a more valuable asset on the night than Bertie's guile and combativeness. On such judgements can matches hinge, though not necessarily in *direct* consequence of the deductive process.

Further complicating matters, Celtic's task would be doubly difficult as the visitors' forward line was now restored to full strength by the return of Trivic and Pusibric. Ironically, first-leg scorer Stanic was one of the men asked to stand down to accommodate the returning stars.

Vojvodina might well have put the tie *beyond* Celtic in a nerve-jangling first half which came uncomfortably close to altering the course of European football history. Their play was sharp, slick and incisive, while Celtic, by contrast, stuttered, stumbled and groped frantically for their true form. After only five minutes, the 'Slavs sliced their way into the Celtic penalty area and the ball ran through to Pusibric, dangerously isolated on the six-yard line. To the crowd's enormous relief and Celtic's great good fortune, the reinstated striker snatched at the early chance and his left-foot shot screwed harmlessly past the post. What a let-off! Such menace continued throughout that unhappy first half, during which the fitful home attacks were comfortably contained and the huge crowd died a thousand deaths of silent apprehension. Goalkeeper Ilya Pantelic swaggered around his area, dealing almost contemptuously with anything Celtic threw at him, which, in truth, was not very much. Centre-half Brzic infuriated the crowd, wasting valuable time by passing back to Pantelic at every opportunity. Somehow Celtic survived, but survival was not enough and unless there was to be a dramatic revival in the second half, it seemed the great European adventure would end right there and then in the most disappointing circumstances, without even much of a fight. *This* was not the *Celtic* way and the fans were finding it hard to take.

Amidst much half-time gloom and despondency, Jock Stein refused to panic. Despite the fact that Vojvodina had seriously threatened to kill the contest, he spent the interval convincing his crestfallen players that they had it in them to turn things around. He urged full-backs Craig and Gemmell to overlap at every opportunity and demanded that Murdoch, too, begin to carry the fight to the 'Slavs. This, however, was only what they should have been doing anyway, when what was really required was something out of the ordinary. What could Stein produce? His masterstroke was to have Celtic line up for the second half with Hughes alongside Johnstone on the right flank. The two appeared almost comical, so great was the physical contrast as they stood together, *but this was no joke* - the objective was to confuse the well-drilled Vojvodina defence and the cunning ploy worked a treat. Right from the whistle, Celtic roared into attack and at last the siege was on. Brzic and co. were soon on the ropes, as wave upon wave of green-shirted attackers bore down on their goal, where Pantelic, so maddeningly cocky in the first half, was not looking very clever now.

Photograph courtesy of Evening Times/Herald

Billy McNeill's stunning winner against Vojvodina.

Just when it seemed that the 'Slavs might weather the storm and frustrate the valiant fightback, Celtic scored to level the aggregate and relieve some of the mounting pressure. Gemmell, the villain of the first leg, following his boss's half-time instructions to the letter, charged down the left and sent over a fast, tantalising cross which lured Pantelic out of his goal. *It was a bad decision.* Fatally overstretched, he failed to gather cleanly. As the ball spun from his grasp, it landed at the quicksilver feet of Stevie Chalmers, who gleefully whipped it into the net. The roar of uncorked relief might have been heard in Novi Sad itself! Inspired, Celtic went for the kill. Pantelic, chastened now and altogether more sombre, kept his reeling side in the game with a series of fantastic saves, first from Johnstone, then Chalmers and a Gemmell drive was deflected high into the air by a defender. It seemed certain to drop into the net but instead just cleared the bar. All this time, Celtic were aware that Vojvodina had been 2-0 down to Atletico in their Madrid play-off, were reduced to nine men, but had still come back from the dead to win 3-2. Clearly, these were no quitters!

As the minutes ticked by, all too fast for Celtic hearts, it looked as though the pre-designated play-off in Rotterdam would be required to settle the issue. Rattled defenders kicked the ball anywhere in their desperation to clear the lines, resulting in a series of late Celtic corners, the last with barely a minute remaining. Charlie Gallagher trotted over to take it on the right, shaped to knock it short to Johnstone, then hesitated. The crowd, agonisingly aware of the lack of time, bayed at Gallagher's apparent dithering ... but Charlie knew *exactly* what he was doing. After all, wasn't this precisely what he had been picked for? He had spotted Billy McNeill setting himself up for a late run and decided that it was now or never. Sensing Gallagher's intention, Stevie Chalmers ran out of the area, happily drawing two defenders with him, to allow McNeill a clear run. As the perfectly-struck corner kick arced high into the glare of the Parkhead floodlights, Chalmers suddenly doubled back into the box, in the process blocking Pantelic's path, no doubt accidentally. Stevie's clever ploy actually made no material difference, as the 'keeper had again crucially misjudged the flight of the ball, which was clearly swinging well out of his reach. 'Caesar', on the other hand had judged his run to perfection and rose like an avenging angel to steer a looping header high into the postage-stamp corner, over even the despairing grasp of left-half Nesticki, stationed at the post. The exultant roar that thundered around Celtic Park had not yet reached its crescendo when the referee blew for time up, dismissing Vojvodina's desperate claims that Pantelic had been fouled and barely allowing the frantic 'Slavs time to centre the ball. Yes, it was that close!

Amongst the many glorious Parkhead nights of a magical era, few, if any, equalled the crackling atmosphere of that night for sheer tension and drama - certainly none surpassed it! The relief and exhilaration which swept around Celtic Park in its wake was still apparent when Queen's Park were entertained the following Saturday, 11th March, in the third round of the Scottish Cup. Tommy Gemmell, once more reverting to his familiar role of 'Clown Prince', gifted Queen's a goal of a start within fifteen seconds, turning a low cross from the amateurs' winger, Watson, past Ronnie Simpson from point-blank range. Big Tam thought it was hilarious, throwing his head back in a hearty laugh, but the fans probably found it easier to see the funny side after Gemmell had made amends with a seventh minute equaliser. Celtic then eased into the old routine, producing a wonderful display of carefree (though, at times, unbelievably careless), attacking football. By half-time, Chalmers, Wallace and Murdoch had taken the score to 4-2, Neil Hopper having had the audacity to bag a second goal for the 'Spiders' on the half-hour mark. Adding insult to injury, Hopper fairly set the cat among the pigeons with his own second and Queen's Park's third one minute into the second forty-five. The ominous spectre of complacency seemed to loom as Queen's gave it their all, perhaps getting an

Photograph courtesy of Evening Times/Herald

Triumphant relief as the final whistle sounds victory over the dangerous 'Slavs.

Superstar Sean Connery displays some fancy footwork before the Queen's Park Scottish Cup tie at Celtic Park, 11th March, 1967 (Above).

This time it's nifty headwork by Willie Wallace, converting a Steve Chalmers cross for goal number three of the 5-3 victory (Below).

unexpected whiff of giant-killing in their nostrils, until Bobby Lennox restored some sanity to the proceedings, sealing the tie for Celtic with a fifth goal in eighty-four minutes. Setting aside Celtic's occasional suicidal tendencies, the most controversial moment of a sometimes crazy match featured (surprise, surprise) Jimmy Johnstone. Midway through the second half, Jimmy's patience snapped when he was felled by the umpteenth 'robust' tackle from his shadow for the day, full-back Gilmour and the wee man shaped unmistakably to butt his assailant in the face. The referee missed the incident but Jock Stein didn't and he immediately pulled Johnstone off. As he left the field, 'Jinky' appeared to make a remark to Stein in the dugout, before sprinting off down the tunnel. Whatever Jimmy said incensed the manager, who sprang out of his seat and lumbered off in hot pursuit of his 'prodigal son', his face a mask of rage. Not for the first time, the tiny winger had overstepped the bounds of Stein's patience. The penalty for this latest indiscretion was a club fine and a one-week ban.

So it was that the fiery redhead was absent from the team to face Dunfermline at home the following Saturday, his place going to John Hughes, at the start of a punishing run of four league games in the space of nine days. The 3-2 scoreline that day misleadingly suggests a close match, which it certainly was *not*. Steve Chalmers nodded Celtic into the lead with a close-in header in only three minutes and although Alex Ferguson snatched a twentieth minute equaliser, Celtic simply swarmed back upfield, exerting immediate pressure which produced a penalty kick, duly converted by Gemmell, just two minutes later. Willie Wallace effectively wrapped up the points with a third shortly before the interval. Continuing the kind of scoring form which would eventually set him on the road to Ibrox, Ferguson's second, three minutes from time, while having no material effect on the outcome of the match, took the aggregate score for the four Celtic/Dunfermline meetings over the season (the two-leg League Cup quarter-final plus home and away league fixtures) to a remarkable and highly-entertaining 17-10 in favour of Celtic! You could get very long odds indeed on such a scoring rate nowadays, a clear reflection of the vastly changed priorities of the modern game. 'Jinky' was reinstated for the rearranged visit of Falkirk two days later, with Charlie Gallagher dropping out to accommodate the return of Bertie Auld and Bobby Lennox also making way for Hughes to cross over to the left flank. Such typical positional and personnel switching had no disruptive effect on the conveyor belt of goals, which continued unabated. Chalmers and Auld did the opening damage in the twenty-fifth and twenty-ninth minutes, then came the customary killer burst of three second-half strikes inside eight minutes from Hughes, Gemmell (pen.) and a second from Chalmers to round things off in the seventy-fourth.

The stiffest test of this arduous schedule came against Hearts at Tynecastle on Saturday, 25th March. Granted, this was not the fluent, potent Hearts outfit which had picked up so much silverware around the turn of the decade, but their Gorgie Road ground was still, traditionally, one of the toughest of venues. Given Celtic's demanding workload, the ever-mounting pressure as they chased further unprecedented success on three fronts and the almost inevitable onset of staleness amongst the squad, it would have been quite understandable for them to slip up here - and maybe a draw would have been acceptable in some quarters. The more so as the game was played in an incessant downpour, which turned the pitch into a stamina-sapping quagmire. Not a bit of it! Not *this* Celtic! Not *that* year! Once the inevitable early Hearts pressure had been absorbed, it was one-way traffic towards Jim Cruickshank in the maroons' goal and it came as no surprise when Bertie Auld finally broke the deadlock with a low drive three minutes before the Bovril. Just after the hour mark, Willie Wallace blasted a glorious twenty-yard free-kick through a gap in the defensive wall and past Cruickshank before he could blink, punishing his former mates and sending the saturated support behind the Hearts goal into raptures. Then Gemmell gave the drookit hordes a special going-away present with a typical thunderbolt penalty five minutes from the end. Despite the relentless drenching endured, the only real dampener for the fans was the enforced substitution of Murdoch by Lennox, 'Murdie' having sustained an injury which was to keep him sidelined for the next four games. Jock Stein, who always seemed to have a couple of aces up his sleeve, would have to shuffle the pack again and deal himself another winning hand.

The tough nine-day slog came to an end at Firhill on Monday, 27th March. Stein resolved the Murdoch problem by exploiting Wallace's versatility (what a wonderful asset 'Wispy' was proving to be!), pulling the chunky forward back into midfield to fill Bobby's 'engine room' role. Charlie Gallagher returned at inside-right, Bobby Lennox played from the start and it was Bertie Auld's turn to drop out again. A remarkable crowd of 30,000 crammed the 'Jags'' Maryhill home - routine testimony to the unparalleled pulling power of the 'Stein Machine' - ***and they were richly rewarded as Lennox claimed the honour of notching up Celtic's hundredth league goal of the season four minutes from the break.*** There was a slight hiccup as John Flanagan equalised for Thistle seven minutes into the second half, but sanity was restored after a further seven, Steve Chalmers edging the 'Bhoys' back in front. Taking his cue for the seven-minute scoring interval, Willie Wallace strode forward from his deep position into more familiar territory to rifle home Celtic's third and Chalmers added his own second near the end to take the score to a satisfying 4-1 and bring the four-on-the-trot tally to 15-3. With hindsight, maybe it wasn't such a punishing programme after all. Certainly, it wasn't *Celtic* who were being punished!

Chapter Five

The Glory Run: Homing in on Lisbon.

At last the heavy grounds of winter gave way to the firmer going of spring:

Harold Wilson's Labour Government was in the middle of a six-year term and a group of London office girls popularised the topical catch-phrase, 'I'm Backing Britain', by carrying shopping bags emblazoned with the patriotic slogan. Wilson was winding the nation up for another attempt to have the U.K. admitted to the Common Market - subsequently to become known as the E.E.C. (European Economic Community) and latterly, simply E.C. as the aims became increasingly political - an attempt which was vetoed by France's rather hostile and aloof President, General Charles de Gaulle, on the grounds that Britain's 'Special Relationship' with the United States 'prevented them from thinking like good Europeans'.

In the world of sport, the American golfer Gay Brewer won the U.S. Masters, depriving Jack Nicklaus of a 'hat-trick' of victories, the great man having triumphed at Augusta for the previous two years in addition to donning his first Green Jacket in 1963. There would be three more Masters titles for the 'Golden Bear' over the next nineteen years as he staked his claim to all-time greatness. At home, the Grand National on 8th April was won by 100/1 outsider Foinavon, ridden by Johnny Buckingham, in what was surely one of the most amazing episodes in the chequered and often controversial history of the classic race. In the wake of an almighty pile-up of fallen, baulked and riderless horses at the twenty-third fence, Foinavon was so far adrift of the field that Buckingham was able to steer his mount gingerly through the mêlée, over the offending hurdle and then put a further two fences between himself and the others before the survivors could regroup and pursue him. By then, all Buckingham had to do was keep Foinavon upright and safely negotiate the five remaining fences to record a famous and unlikely victory.

Celtic, still without the injured Bobby Murdoch, were nevertheless not expected to make proverbial fools of themselves when they faced Clyde in the Scottish Cup semi-final at Hampden on Saturday, 1st

April. This was, however, easily the pride of Rutherglen's best year since winning the national trophy in 1958. They were well on their way to finishing third in the Championship and anyway, nothing could ever be taken for granted in a semi-final. In the event, Clyde let themselves down and never seriously threatened in a surprisingly dull game, the tension of the occasion obviously affecting the players. As chance would have it, Celtic, too, seemed strangely out-of-sorts, never at any time approaching the fluency they had been displaying all season. The nearest they came to scoring was in the eighty-sixth minute, when Lennox wrong-footed the 'Bully Wee' defence to cut the ball back into the path of the inrushing Johnstone. It seemed the wee man must score and he did everything just right, but his net-bound effort appeared to be elbowed over the bar by full-back Soutar. The referee resolutely waved aside the Celtic appeals and the game petered out into the lacklustre goalless draw it probably deserved to be.

For the rematch the following Wednesday evening, Stein relegated Hughes to the bench and fielded an unusual and intriguing left-wing partnership of Gallagher and Auld. Clyde, for their part, dropped future Celt, Harry Hood, in favour of left-winger McFarlane. Belying its semi-final replay status, with all that usually implies, this turned out to be a total anti-climax, as Lennox shot Celtic to the comfort of a second-minute lead and Auld put the result beyond much doubt well before the half-hour mark. Clyde, still tamely offering no more than token resistance, were virtual spectators at a casual Celtic work-out.

Relentless consistency in the league seemed finally to have worn Rangers down as Celtic strode within two points of retaining the title at Fir Park, Motherwell on Saturday, 8th April, with a solid 2-0 win. Second-half goals from a typically-powerful Willie Wallace drive and a fearsome Gemmell penalty, which fairly thundered past Peter McCloy, did the trick and sent the fans home licking their lips in anticipation. The way was now clear for the Champions' Cup semi-final against Dukla Prague, the renowned Czech Army team, with the first leg at Celtic Park the following Wednesday evening.

Dukla arrived in Glasgow with a brilliant football reputation. For all that, they could not boast any household names, save, perhaps, the once-illustrious veteran, Josef Masopust, the brains behind Czechoslovakia's surge to the World Cup Final in Santiago, Chile, five years previously. Then, despite taking the lead, the Czechs had been beaten 3-1 by holders, Brazil, largely due to ghastly blunders by goalkeeper Walter Schroif, who gifted Vava two simple goals before Amarildo, the 'White Pele', wrapped it up with a blistering shot from near the bye-line (Neilly Mochan-style!) late in the game. Of course, the legendary, dazzling, free-flowing football of the Brazilian maestros had a little to do with it as well.

Billy McNeill would remember Masopust from the qualifying ties for that World Cup. The Celtic captain had played for Scotland in Bratislava in 1961, when the Czechs won comprehensively, 4-0 and again later the same year in the return leg on a wet September Tuesday afternoon (Hampden did not yet have floodlights). On that memorable occasion, one of the most talented and exciting Scotland sides in recent history, featuring the likes of Crerand, Baxter, White, Law and St John, had produced a famous victory, twice coming from behind, to win 3-2. Big Billy was not selected for the ensuing decider in Brussels to determine which country would go to Chile. In those days, *goal average* only came into force if two countries finished a qualifying section with equal points and were still level after extra-time in a neutral play-off. When asked to propose a venue for the showdown, the S.F.A. had optimistically suggested Wembley. The Czechs responded predictably with the Bohemian equivalent of, 'Aye, that'll be right, Jimmy!' and Brussels was duly designated. In the best Scottish World Cup tradition, our tartan heroes, crucially deprived of wingers Scott and Wilson, came within eight minutes of triumph in the face of adversity, as they truly were 'glorious in defeat'. The normally irrepressible Denis Law and principal playmaker, the late, great John 'White Ghost' White of Tottenham, who would be so tragically killed by lightning in his prime a few years later, were tightly shackled by the solid Czech defence. Still, centre-forward, Ian St John somehow contrived to grab two goals against one by Hledik, to take the Scots to the very brink of qualification. Then Scherer went and spoiled the party by rattling home what was, in all honesty, a deserved equaliser in the eighty-second minute. With their resolution broken, the South American dream was shattered as Scotland fatally conceded a further two goals in the first period of extra time. The *Times* rightly summed it up: 'Czechoslovakia will take some stopping in Chile.' They did!

Although Dukla had provided the bulk of that great Czech national side, Masopust was the sole survivor in their ranks and, at 36, even *his* was an aging genius. Nevertheless, they had eliminated the exciting young bucks of Ajax, who had, in turn, dumped Bill Shankly's Liverpool 7-3 on aggregate in the second round, winning by an astonishing 5-1 in the Amsterdam fog before comfortably holding the 'Reds' 2-2 at Anfield. The spellbinding talent of Johann Cruyff, though then still embryonic, was extant enough to confirm that a major new star was rising in the football firmament. Ajax had been devastating against Liverpool, particularly in that first leg - yet Dukla had taken them. Despite this daunting omen, Celtic fans were relaxed with the draw, which had kept them apart from Inter Milan, generally perceived as the main threat, who now faced a 'journey into the unknown' to play Bulgarian Champs, C.S.K.A. Sofia.

A capacity crowd which felt much tighter than the official figure of 75,000 was crammed into Celtic Park on a snell April evening, taut with a kind of dread anticipation. This was uncharted territory and now that it had come down to the crunch, Dukla's awesome reputation loomed large. Perhaps, though, Celtic could exploit their probable inability to cope with the phenomenal Parkhead pace. In the opening minutes, this appeared a forlorn hope, as the Czechs oozed composure and skill. Ronnie Simpson averted a catastrophic start with two smart early

Photograph courtesy of Evening Times/Herald

Jimmy Johnstone bursts clear and is poised for his super strike in the home first leg of the European Cup semi-final against Dukla Prague, 12th April, 1967.

saves. Gradually, however, the initial Dukla menace was neutralised and Celtic roared into life themselves. They looked to have taken the lead when Chalmers headed a Johnstone cut-back powerfully past Czech 'keeper Ivo Viktor - reckoned to be one of the best in Europe - but the referee, to general consternation, disallowed the 'score' on account of 'feet up' by 'Jinky' in winning possession. It was hard to take - but Celtic were to be denied only a few minutes more. As a Wallace drive cannoned off a defender, Johnstone's reaction was swift and devastating. Bursting into the box, instinct outstripping thought by that vital fraction of a second, he killed the awkward dropping ball on his chest and without breaking stride, lifted it delicately over the outrushing Viktor. It was a moment of succulent skill, a flash of rare genius, at which the terracings erupted in joyous bedlam. Surely *that* would break even these tough, military hearts? Defiantly, though, Dukla instantly began to show their true mettle. Where lesser mortals might have panicked, stricken in spectacular fashion and faced with a younger, fitter team, bolstered by a huge, fanatically partisan crowd (much bigger than Dukla were used to at home behind the 'Iron Curtain'), *they* consciously set about slowing the game down with prolonged spells of frustrating possession football, using all their guile and experience to draw Celtic's sting. For the remaining eighteen minutes of that first half, the visitors asserted themselves with a vengeance, inducing the first seeds of doubt in minds to which such a concept was totally alien. This disconcerting Czech comeback was emphatically capped in the very last minute of an increasingly edgy first forty-five. The wily Masopust, sensing, perhaps, premature Celtic relaxation, drifted forward, languidly evading challenges and released a clever reverse pass to inside-left Nederost. McNeill, Clark and Gemmell instinctively converged in unison on the sudden threat at the edge of their area, but only succeeded in getting in each other's way. McNeill's resulting panicky half-clearance simply broke straight back to Nederost, who although grounded, had the presence of mind to stick out a leg and poke the ball to top-scorer Stanislav Strunc, unmarked, onside and only fifteen yards out. Not one to pass up such a gift, the lethal right-winger needed no second bidding and his measured shot beat Simpson low at his right-hand post. These Czechs had come from behind in both legs against Ajax. Now they had done it again. Were Celtic to go down the same road as the Dutchmen?

The tense minutes immediately preceding half-time are generally considered just about the worst time to concede a goal, especially when it is tight and there is a lot at stake. The scoring side get a tremendous lift, whereas the victims are invariably stunned and tend to take only negative thoughts into the dressing room. Realising this and its destructive potential, Jock Stein craftily turned the unfortunate timing of Dukla's strike to Celtic's advantage, strangling at birth any glimmer of despair at the Strunc goal. He was able to convince his players, who by now hung on his every, seemingly-prophetic word, that the worst was behind them; that they had the spirit and ability to overcome this setback and go on to win decisively. Better to concede a goal before half-time, with the opportunity to rationalise the loss and regroup over the

Willie Wallace in hectic goalmouth action against Dukla. 'Wispy's' two second-half strikes gave Celtic the cushion they needed for the tense return in the Juliska Stadium which would be their passport to the historic Lisbon final.

interval, than to lose one early in the second half, when panic might easily set in and allow the opposition to capitalise on their breakthrough without any loss of momentum.

Right from the re-start, then, Celtic seized the initiative again and went at Dukla (who had probably expected the Scots' heads still to be down) with renewed purpose and vigour. Surely the relentless pace of these youthful Celts (only Simpson and Chalmers were over 30) would prove too much for their aging adversaries, half of whom had to be considered veterans. It certainly seemed so as, after fourteen minutes of sustained pressure, Celtic got their noses in front again. Gemmell, forsaking the customary cultured build-up, punted a long clearance deep into Dukla territory, no doubt hoping the change of tack would find them off guard and create confusion. As the ball bounced high and awkwardly into the penalty area, the Czech back-men were caught in an ecstasy of fumbling as Willie Wallace moved in. Keeping his eye on the ball and judging its flight to perfection, even as it became a blur against the glare of the floodlights in the night sky, 'Wispy' chased into the box and stabbed a solid right-footer past the stranded Viktor, who had finally decided, too late, to come off his line. There was to be no way back for Dukla this time. It is doubtful whether the entire Czech Army could have contained those Scottish stormtroopers. Wave after remorseless wave of Celtic attacks stretched the visitors to breaking point, pulling them this way and that, until, just six minutes after opening his European account, Wallace snatched a priceless second. He produced a burst of blistering pace to collect a return pass from Murdoch, but the move was thwarted by the hand of a desperate defender, an offence which would automatically warrant a red card these days but did not even merit a booking in 1967. (Not that the referee could have produced a card, anyway, since the system was not introduced until the 'seventies.) The resulting free-kick was plumb in front of the Dukla goal, just over twenty yards out, seemingly tailor-made for a Gemmell blockbuster. But the wily Bertie Auld sensed that it was going to take a touch of subtlety, gamesmanship if you like, to crack such an experienced rearguard from a dead-ball situation. With Murdoch and Wallace ranged on either side of him, the scheming inside-man shuffled forward and stooped over the ball, as if to reposition it. The well-rehearsed ploy induced the desired momentary and fatal relaxation in the Czechs. Hooding his intentions with the hunched posture, Auld tapped the ball gently to his right, where Wallace crashed a low drive past the flaccid wall and into Viktor's net before the 'keeper could move. It was one of the smartest set-piece 'cons' ever!

How Celtic failed to add to their tally in the remaining quarter of the game shall forever remain a mystery. Wallace was cruelly robbed of a momentous European début 'hat-trick' by the woodwork. As a Chalmers cross reached him through a ruck of players, he stretched out a leg with the striker's instinct and deflected the ball upwards and goalwards. All around froze as the reflex effort screwed off the face of the bar and was scrambled to safety. Amidst other such narrow squeaks, Dukla somehow managed to stumble uncertainly through that Parkhead cauldron to the merciful sanctuary of the final whistle without further loss.

The matching moods of justifiable optimism in the Celtic camp and amongst the supporters were nevertheless rightly tinged with caution. *Yes*, Dukla had set out their attacking stall during that first half and, save for the one highly-preventable incursion, had been routinely kept at arm's length. It seemed inconceivable that Celtic could succumb by three goals (remember that away goals did not then count double in the event of a tie) to a side they had so comprehensively outplayed in the end. Yet, ominously, no British team had ever managed to clear the semi-final hurdle in that great competition. Hibernian, Manchester United (twice), Rangers, Dundee and Liverpool had all faltered at the penultimate stage. Could Celtic possibly succeed where *they* had failed? Could Jock Stein and his shock-troops take that giant step on the road to soccer immortality? The away leg against Dukla Prague on 25th April would tell.

There is no rest, they say, for the wicked; nor, it would seem, for the successful footballer. Four of Celtic's European heroes had been selected to play for Scotland against the 'Auld Enemy' at Wembley in the Home International Championship just three days later. The match on Saturday, 15th April would be of special significance: U.E.F.A. had decreed that the combined Home International series of seasons 1966/67 and 1967/68 would count as a British qualifying section for the European Championship (then known as the European Nations' Cup) to be held in Italy in June 1968. Given that both Scotland and England had already recorded routine wins against Northern Ireland and Wales, the clashes between the two at Wembley and Hampden were already taking on the look of section deciders. A further touch of piquancy lay in the fact that England were still basking in the previous year's World Cup glory, since when they remained unbeaten in any international. A good performance under the twin towers was, therefore, even more important than usual - and that's saying something!

For Scotland boss, Bobby Brown, it was his first match in charge of the national side. He had promptly awarded Ronnie Simpson a fairytale first cap at the age of 36, making him Scotland's oldest-ever international débutant. He had also selected Tommy Gemmell, Jimmy Johnstone and Bobby Lennox. Then, when Johnstone was forced to call off with a knock sustained in the Dukla game, Brown simply lifted the 'phone to Parkhead again to draft in Willie Wallace. 'Wispy' had played for John Prentice's side in the previous year's thrilling Hampden encounter with England's soon-to-be World Champions, a match which the wingerless Sassenachs won 4-3. Wallace, then with Hearts, had acquitted himself well, but the undoubted star in dark blue was little Jimmy Johnstone, who had sparkled and scored two magnificent goals. 'Jinky' had given a tantalising glimpse that day of what might have been over the years if only a certain implacable section of the Scottish support had opened their hearts to the wee man and made him feel more welcome in the team.

Brown had also bestowed a début cap on the youngest player afield, another man with loose Parkhead connections, Celtic-daft Glaswegian, Jim McCalliog. The Sheffield Wednesday centre-forward had joined Chelsea straight from school and been a great success with Tommy Docherty's exciting young lions at Stamford Bridge before moving on to Sheffield and helping guide Wednesday to the F.A. Cup Final of 1966, knocking out the 'Pensioners' 3-1 in the semi-final on the way, *the* shock result of the competition. Sadly for Jim, he was to finish on the wrong end of an epic comeback in the final itself, as Everton overhauled a 2-0 deficit with two snap goals by unheralded Cornishman, Mike Trebilcock (a surprise selection in place of out-of-form England internationalist Fred Pickering) and a late winner from winger Derek Temple.

They also say it's an ill wind that blows no good and the Wembley match meant a well-earned rest for Celtic's non participants, any of whom could easily have played. With the exception of Bertie Auld, who had won three full caps in his first stint at Celtic and Charlie Gallagher, an Eire internationalist, every other member of Celtic's regular first-team squad (Simpson, Craig, Gemmell, Murdoch, McNeill, Clark, Johnstone, Wallace, McBride, Lennox, Chalmers and Hughes) played for Scotland between 1966 and 1968.

Celtic's next game was the postponed league match with Aberdeen at Parkhead the following Wednesday, 19th April. A win would almost certainly clinch the league title, on *goal difference* at least. However, 'Dons' manager Eddie Turnbull had other ideas, and his motto for this Cup Final 'rehearsal' seemed to be, 'They shall not pass', as his men held Celtic to a frustrating 0-0 draw, preventing the uncorking of the victory champagne. In this game, for only the second time that season (the first had been the 4-0 win over St Johnstone at Muirton on 14th

January), Stein fielded the eleven who would eventually gain immortality as the 'Lisbon Lions'. Throughout a season of constant chopping and changing for a variety of reasons, physical, tactical and form-driven, players such as Willie O'Neill, Charlie Gallagher and John Hughes had enjoyed extended runs in the first team. O'Neill had finally lost his place to a reinstated Jim Craig at the turn of the year, Auld had recovered from injury to reclaim his midfield spot from Charlie Gallagher towards the end of the season and the 'Bear' finally ran out of steam against Dukla at Parkhead. Looking overweight and cumbersome against the Czechs, he was completely ineffectual and Bobby Lennox returned, razor-sharp, to see the season out. After all the permutations, *the* team had finally emerged.

Celtic had the luxury of a free Saturday before the Dukla return in Prague's Juliska Stadium on Tuesday, 25th April. Stein's only change from the first leg was Lennox for the jaded Hughes. For Dukla, Knebort replaced Dvorak in midfield. During the obligatory pre-match ceremonials and photo-calls, Celtic faces were tense and strained, taut with grim determination. In contrast to the seething, sell-out crowd which had been shoe-horned into the vast bowl of Celtic Park, fewer than 20,000 hardy souls (including, of course, the inevitable healthy band of travelling Celtic stalwarts) were scattered around the bleak Juliska. Many of the Czechs congregated on the grassy bank which formed one side of the stadium were in uniform, emphasising Dukla's military status.

One wonders, with the benefit of hindsight, how many of these young men of Prague were destined to be caught up in the altogether more sinister events which rocked their capital city just sixteen months later, when, in August 1968, Soviet tanks rumbled into Wenceslaus Square to quell an attempted breakaway by the revolutionary Czech government of Alexander Dubcek. The courageous, if politically naive, leader was summarily deposed, replaced by a Moscow puppet and his bold, idealistic 'Prague Spring' régime ruthlessly suppressed. The strength of Czech bitterness towards their oppressors was epitomised by a twenty-year-old student named Jan Palach. Emulating the Buddhist monks who protested similarly at the Vietnam War, Palach 'torched' himself in the Square and is still regarded as a martyr in Czech folklore. These grisly events drew a typically principled response from Celtic in the form of a protest to U.E.F.A. that Western clubs should not, under the circumstances, be obliged to compete against teams from Warsaw Pact countries. Having already been drawn against Ferencvaros, of Hungary, then another Soviet satellite state, in what would probably have been **the** *tie of the first round of the 1968/69 competition, the Parkhead board were risking the need for a humiliating stand-down if their protest fell on deaf ears. It was, however, a measure of Celtic's standing in Europe* *at the time that the wide backing they received led to a segregated re-draw which prompted the blanket withdrawal of Eastern Bloc clubs.*

Back in the Juliska, which might charitably be described as Scottish Second Division standard, Celtic set out to hold what they had. Getting behind the ball en masse, they allowed Dukla to make all the running, confident of their ability to keep the Czechs at bay. Throughout the ninety minutes, Ronnie Simpson was called upon to make one flying save from Nederost, brilliantly tipping the ball over the bar for a corner. The only other near thing came midway through the second half, when the same player scorned a good chance by hurriedly shooting into the side net, having been given a rare glimpse of goal by the watertight Parkhead defence. By that time, however, it was all over bar the shouting. It was clear that Celtic, this unfamiliar Celtic, playing with only Steve Chalmers up front, were going to make British football history. Jock Stein later often confessed to embarrassment at the negative defensive tactics he laid down for his team that day, but surely this was a classic case of the end justifying the means. The radiant faces of his players as they capered around on a cold Prague afternoon and the boundless joy generated back home by the transmission of the jubilant scenes to a tea-time audience, *were* that justification.

Domestic matches on the Saturday before, or after, midweek European ties are notoriously difficult. Before competing in Europe, players are inevitably rather preoccupied with the forthcoming contest, perhaps even subconsciously holding back a little to avoid injury. After the big event, they are likely to be physically drained, mentally exhausted and either emotionally high or low. For Celtic, all these factors were magnified on their return from Prague. They had not won just any old European tie: *against all odds, they had qualified for the European Cup Final itself*. Under the circumstances it would have been difficult enough to gear up for a bread and butter league match. How much *more* demanding then, only four days after their 'landmark' achievement in Czechoslovakia, to be confronted by Aberdeen in the Scottish Cup Final at Hampden Park?

Along with Kilmarnock and Dundee United, Aberdeen shared the considerable distinction of being unbeaten by Celtic all season, having drawn both league meetings, 1-1 at Pittodrie and 0-0 at Celtic Park just ten days before the final. In contrast to Celtic's relatively straightforward cup run, eluding First Division opposition until the semi-final, the 'Dons' had had it tough - or so it had seemed on paper! In the first round, they were drawn at home to Dundee, always a tough proposition, especially in the cup. However, with Jimmy 'Snakehips' Smith, one of the many Glasgow boys stolen away from under the noses of the 'Old Firm' by Aberdeen's legendary scout, Bobby Calder, turning in a magnificent performance, the men in red ran out easy 5-0 winners. St Johnstone faced the unenviable task of following Dundee to Pittodrie for the second round and they, too, found themselves on the wrong end of a 5-0 hammering. It was much closer, though, at Easter Road in the quarter-final, when it took a late equaliser by right-half Frank Munro to earn Aberdeen a midweek Pittodrie replay, which they won comfortably 3-0. The semi-final draw had then paired Aberdeen with Dundee United in a 'New Firm' derby at Dens Park. In a grim tussle, the sides were narrowly separated by an own-goal from the unfortunate Doug Millar of United. Aberdeen made no attempt to reproduce the fluent football which had carried them impressively thus far in the competition, relying on sheer power to see off United in a backs-to-the-wall operation similar to Celtic's in Prague. Clearly, then, Celtic faced a daunting task in their bid to stay on course for the unprecedented domestic 'Grand Slam' which was now tantalisingly within their grasp. So soon after their physical and emotional exertions in Czechoslovakia, they were being asked to regroup, blunt a dangerous, free-scoring attack and break down one of the tightest defences in the land.

Aberdeen were dealt a cruel blow when their inspirational boss, Eddie Turnbull , was unable to travel to Hampden, being confined to his pre-match headquarters in the Gleneagles Hotel with a severe stomach complaint. Perhaps the gods had decided to smile on Celtic that fateful morning of 29th April, 1967. Meanwhile, Jock Stein had been deliberating over his team selection, swithering whether to include Steve Chalmers, who had run himself into the ground in Czechoslovakia, or to rest him and bring in John Hughes. Perhaps letting his heart rule his head, Stein decided that Stevie had earned his place in the final and stuck with the Prague eleven.

A warm spring sun shone on Hampden Park as the colourful throng descended on the famous old ground. Proud northern 'louns', confidently sporting their red favours and hoisting their *Wee Alickie* mascots, mingled happily in a sea of green as the rival fans streamed unsegregated along Cathcart Road before splitting out and massing separately in their respective sectors - 'Dons' on the Mount Florida slopes, 'Tims' at the traditional (King's Park) 'Celtic End'. The main Hampden approaches, Aitkenhead Road, Prospecthill Road and Somerville Drive, were a riot of colour, vibrant with the din of mounting Cup Final fever and by kick-off time a seething crowd of 126,102 was settling down to watch the following line-ups do battle:

CELTIC :- Simpson; Craig & Gemmell; Murdoch, McNeill & Clark; Johnstone, Wallace, Chalmers, Auld & Lennox.

ABERDEEN :- Clark; Whyte & Shewan; Munro, McMillan & Petersen; Wilson, Smith, Storrie, Melrose & Johnston.

The Aberdeen captain, Harry Melrose, was facing Celtic in a Scottish Cup Final for the third time in six years, having won and lost with Dunfermline in the finals of 1961 and 1965 respectively. Right from the off, he was marked down for another runner-up medal, as Celtic roared onto the attack, kicking into a stiff breeze, their sustained pressure forcing Bobby Clark to look sharp on several occasions. To relieve the siege, Aberdeen's bulky centre-forward, Jim Storrie, ex-Airdrie, who had been signed earlier in the season from Leeds United and had played against Liverpool in the 1965 F.A. Cup Final, which Leeds lost 2-0, tried to surprise Ronnie Simpson from ridiculously far out. Twice he tried, and twice 'Faither' calmly watched his optimistic efforts sail harmlessly over the bar. Celtic, however, *did* present Aberdeen with one scoring chance in the first half. Winger Jimmy Wilson collected the ball in the centre circle, raced forward as defenders backed off him, but failed to exploit the gap which suddenly materialised. He seemed to lose his nerve, passed, instead of having a go himself and the chance was lost. Celtic turned the screw as half-time approached. In forty-one minutes, Lennox took a corner short to Auld, collected the return pass and danced past two defenders before hammering the ball across the face of the goal from the bye-line. Willie Wallace reacted quicker than anyone else to stab the ball right-footed into the net at the near post. Already it looked like curtains for Aberdeen. Three minutes into the second half, came the killer blow. Johnstone and Chalmers, presumably on half-time instructions, had confused the Aberdeen rearguard by switching places, Chalmers operating wide on the right, with Johnstone going through the middle. The switch paid off early. As Chalmers flicked the ball into Johnstone's path in the inside-right channel, 'Jinky' chased it to the goal-line and pulled back a tempting cross. A grateful Willie Wallace, completely unmarked only eight yards out, had time to steady himself before smashing an unstoppable drive past the stranded Clark.

With defeat now staring them squarely in the face, Aberdeen began to open out, producing some of their most enterprising football. Realising the futility of further dour defence, they started to bring the gifted Smith into the game and the youngster responded by releasing Storrie through the middle with only Simpson to beat. Big Jim shot powerfully enough, but the veteran goalie pulled off one of those typically graceful diving saves of his to beat the ball out to safety.

Thereafter, Celtic were mainly content to contain Aberdeen with neat possession football, pressing forward only spasmodically, as and when the flow dictated. These 'guerrilla' tactics almost paid off in further goals as Wallace came close to his 'hat-trick' with a shot which whistled over the bar, while both Lennox and Chalmers had good efforts saved. In the last flurry of action, by which time it would have been purely academic anyway, Aberdeen all but scored. Wilson's cross from the right found its way through to the big Dane, Petersen, sliding in at the far post and he nudged the ball towards an empty net from no more than six yards out. This must have been a day, though, when Ronnie Simpson was *destined* not to be beaten! Just as the consolation goal appeared inevitable, he seemed to materialise out of thin air to boot the ball clear, right off the line. It was an astonishing little incident, one of many in a truly remarkable season for the 'born again' 'keeper. In addition to having become his country's oldest-ever international débutant, he had been voted *Footballer of the Year* by the Scottish Football Writers and now he had won his first Scottish Cup winner's medal to go alongside the two F.A. Cup badges collected with the successful Newcastle United sides of 1952 and 1955.

As a footnote to this final, season 1968/69 saw Aberdeen transfer Jimmy Smith for £100,000 to that same Newcastle United, where he became a firm favourite with the passionate Geordie fans and went on to play twice for Scotland. Celtic subsequently had him on loan for a month in 1975/76 after a serious knee injury had sidelined him for a lengthy spell, but a relapse dashed mutual hopes of a permanent move, without even a run in the top team.

So Celtic's triumphant march continued as Billy McNeill again held the Scottish Cup on high, 'crowning' himself in the process when the lid fell off and hit him on the head. Sadly, the euphoric support was that day denied the once-traditional victory parade, the S.F.A. and Scottish League having banned laps of honour following a pitch invasion by enraged Rangers fans as Celtic showed off the League Cup *to their own supporters* after winning 2-1 in the 1965 final. That punitive ban remained infuriatingly in force throughout Jock Stein's rich stewardship at Celtic Park.

Steve Chalmers and the Aberdeen defence watch in apparent disbelief at Willie Wallace's stunning opener in the Scottish Cup Final, 29th April, 1967 (Above).

The aftermath, as 'Wispy' does a jig of delight and his team-mates react in their various ways. Billy McNeill seems to be making an early dash for the dressing room (Below).

Photograph courtesy of Evening Times/Herald

The killer blow in the Scottish Cup Final as Wallace rifles home the second from Johnstone's perfect cut-back. The goal-line defender seems to be looking hopefully at Bobby Lennox's positioning – but it was a forlorn hope!

Photograph courtesy of Evening Times/Herald

It looks a goal all the way – but this was Ronnie Simpson's super, point-blank Cup Final save from Aberdeen centre, Jim Storrie.

Focus then switched back to the Championship, which could be tied up at Parkhead the following Wednesday, 3rd May, in a rearranged fixture against Dundee United, who remained the only side to inflict the indignity of domestic defeat on Celtic that season, having won the first league meeting 3-2 at Tannadice the previous Hogmanay. A bumper crowd of 44,000 rolled up to Celtic Park on a balmy spring evening fully expecting to see that particular blot on the record comprehensively expunged. Statistically, though, setting aside the obvious satisfaction *that* would afford, revenge was not what really mattered, but the two title-clinching points a victory would secure; and with the coming Saturday's match at Ibrox, nerve-ends were sure to be more than a little frayed if the league wasn't in the bag by then. A solid, dispassionate home performance, then, was the order of the day to render the Rangers game a purely prestige affair.

Unfortunately, the visitors' manager, Jerry Kerr, had no intention of serving the title up to Celtic on a Tayside plate. Perhaps, as an ex-Ranger, he was of a mind to keep his former club in with a shout; but more likely he was determined to prove that United's home win had been no fluke. In any event, the 'Arabs' erected a white wall in front of goalkeeper Sandy Davie and Celtic battered fruitlessly against it until the twenty-seventh minute. When Lennox was pulled down in the box, Tommy Gemmell delivered his usual net-bulger from the spot and that was that until half-time.

Stein had finally rested Chalmers, switching Wallace to centre-forward. Hughes had returned at outside-left, with Lennox moving inside and Auld dropping out to accommodate Charlie Gallagher once again at inside-right. Perhaps so many changes up front had unsettled the team, for they signally failed to stamp their authority and ram home their advantage in the usual manner after the break. United, by contrast, continued to play as if it was *their* Cup Final and Billy Hainey, a strong-running centre, formerly of Partick Thistle, chased down a long ball and slammed a shock equaliser past the advancing Simpson ten minutes after the restart. This looked to be a temporary blip as, six minutes later, Celtic went in front again and it seemed as though fresh green and white ribbons could be put on order for the trophy. Willie Wallace had 'done a Hainey' on a no-chance ball deep into the Dundee box. Centre-half Walter Smith (whatever became of *him ?*) left it to his 'keeper, but the never-say-die 'Wispy' lunged in to poke home. The joyous victory anthems rolling around the ground were stifled, though, when veteran inside-left Dennis Gillespie ghosted in at the back post to convert a hard Orjan Persson cross for United's second equaliser of the night - and a deathly hush accompanied what proved to be a paralysing winner just three minutes later. Incredibly, the Tannadice men had done it again, completing a chastening double over the otherwise all-conquering Parkhead thoroughbreds. Adding insult to injury, the strike which had put retention of the Championship onto the back burner had been a gift, as Jim Craig made a hash of a pass-back and winger Graham, presented with a clear run in on goal, made no mistake.

United's Parkhead 'smash-and-grab' gave Rangers double cause for celebration. On the same evening as that unexpected league reprieve, they defeated Bulgarians, Slavia Sofia, 1-0 at Ibrox to book their place in the European Cup-Winners' Cup Final, scheduled for Nuremberg on 31st May. It was a magnificent achievement, not only for Rangers themselves but also for Glasgow and Scotland, who now had two representatives in the major European finals. Indeed, Kilmarnock almost made it an amazing 1967 Scottish 'hat-trick', only losing narrowly to Leeds United in the semi-final of the Fairs' Cup, forerunner of the present-day U.E.F.A. Cup. The Rangers support was filled with renewed hope. Had Celtic finally shot their bolt? Suddenly, Saturday couldn't come fast enough for the boys in blue. Whoever said, 'What a difference a day makes'?

In marked contrast to the Scottish Cup Final of seven days earlier, the potential league decider was played in torrential rain. Glasgow awoke to leaden skies and by early that afternoon of 6th May, the heavens had opened, as if in premature impartial mourning for whichever would be the downhearted half of *this* 'Old Firm' line-up:

RANGERS :- Martin; Johansen & Provan; Jardine, McKinnon & Greig; Henderson, A. Smith, Hynd, D. Smith & Johnston.

CELTIC :- Simpson; Craig & Gemmell; Murdoch, McNeill & Clark; Johnstone, Wallace, Chalmers, Auld & Lennox.

Yes, the soon-to-be 'Lisbon Lions' were on parade again, as they had been for the Cup Final. Indeed, these were exactly the clubs' respective line-ups for their imminent Euro-finals.

Despite the midweek reverse, arithmetic dictated that a draw against their only potential title contenders would be enough to see Celtic re-crowned as Champions, whereas Rangers had to win to keep their revitalised challenge alive. Surely, *this* was the perfect recipe for a classic Glasgow derby!

Due largely to the inclement weather, the game straight away developed into a dour power struggle in which skill had to take a back seat. When the grim deadlock was broken, it was Rangers who seized the crucial initiative through a stunning strike by their discovery of that season, a fresh-faced right-half named Sandy Jardine. Forty minutes of an uncompromising territorial battle had elapsed when the youngster deftly tamed a Willie Johnston pass twenty-two yards out and lashed a glorious drive into the net off the underside of the crossbar. The Copland Road terracing behind Ronnie Simpson erupted in an intimidating frenzy of blue. Within a minute, though, the impromptu 'Teddy Bears' Picnic' was abandoned as parity was restored. Right from the kick-off, their pride wounded, Celtic had roared downfield. Murdoch fed the ball into the Rangers penalty area, triggering an almighty stramash, which ended with Lennox bundling it past Norrie Martin. The scrambled effort came back off a post and it was Jimmy Johnstone who reacted quickest to force the ball over the line. No classic, to be sure, but just the job under the circumstances.

Things remained locked at 1-1 until late in the second half, with neither side able to gain the ascendancy and it looked as though Celtic would probably hold on for the precious point they needed without further incident. Then Jimmy Johnstone decided to take a hand, popping up to dignify proceedings with one of the most memorable goals ever seen at Ibrox. As the rain pounded down, he picked up a throw-in from Steve Chalmers midway inside the Rangers half on the Celtic right. Scuttling over the glaur, the wee man weaved and checked his way past three would-be tacklers, made space on the edge of the box, then turned to unleash a left-foot screamer which scorched high past Martin's despairing right hand into the roof of the 'onion bag'. Bedlam now reigned at the Broomloan end! Little wonder after a goal of such outstanding quality - *surely* it was all over now?

Celtic dug in to resist the inevitable frenzied Rangers onslaught over the remaining quarter of an hour and held out doggedly until misfortune struck nine minutes from the end. When Ronnie Simpson went for a low cross from Henderson, the greasy ball squirmed from his grasp straight to Roger Hynd, Rangers' makeshift centre-forward, who slid the windfall home from six yards. Justice prevailed, though, and moments later the Celtic legions were proclaiming a second consecutive League Championship.

Curiously, the expressions on the Champs' faces as they trudged off at the end were more suited to a league just *lost*, rather than won. A celebrated photograph of the time shows Bobby Murdoch, head bowed, preoccupied and Willie Wallace gazing distraughtly at the camera. Paradoxically, only Willie Johnston of Rangers manages a smile as he leaves the pitch arm-in-arm with Bobby Lennox. Jim Craig has the haunted look of a patient in his own dentist's waiting room. Even

Jimmy Johnstone's wonder goal at Ibrox in the 1966/67 League Championship decider on 6th May leaves Norrie Martin clawing helplessly in mid-air (Above).

Martin is left sprawling in the Ibrox mud with the Rangers defence in varying states of disarray as the Celtic celebrations begin (Below).

allowing for the physically draining conditions, this was surely the most sombre-looking bunch of men who ever clinched a League Championship. Could it be that, with the final domestic hurdle now safely negotiated, the players' minds were suddenly free to focus on the enormity of the greater external challenge that lay ahead? Very probably.

The following Wednesday, Simpson, Gemmell, McNeill, Clark, Johnstone, Lennox and Wallace (as substitute) all played for Scotland in a friendly international against the U.S.S.R., who had finished fourth in the World Cup the previous summer. Sadly, with such a prominent Celtic contingent, the national side was brought back to earth with a bump after the epic victory at Wembley. The Soviets fairly sliced them up and won comfortably 2-0, with goals from Sabo ... and Gemmell! Big Tam contrived to lob Ronnie Simpson perfectly with a twenty-five yard pass-back, failing to check whether the 'keeper had come off his line. Regrettably, he had. Still, it could have been worse - *it might have happened four days earlier!*

Celtic wound up their league programme on Monday, 15th May, with a makeweight, low-key home fixture against Kilmarnock. Long-serving reserve centre-half, John Cushley, quaintly remembered for his rôle as interpreter (being fluent in Spanish) in the abortive 1964 attempt to sign up the aging genius of Alfredo Di Stefano from Real Madrid, as well as for his sterling service whenever called upon to stand in for Billy McNeill, had been transfer-listed and was interesting West Ham United. 'Cush' was drafted in for that final game, largely for the benefit of the 'Hammers', with big Billy inexplicably filling the No 8 shirt. Celtic wore all-green, as they had on that infinitely more atmospheric night against Vojvodina and Stevie Chalmers was again rested. The champions of 1965 were beaten at a canter, with a goal in each half, first Lennox, then Wallace doing the needful and Cushley was duly transferred to Upton Park for £20,000 on 2nd June.

Nothing then remained of the Scottish league season of 1966/67 but to contemplate and admire Celtic's truly formidable record:

Played	Won	Drawn	Lost	For	Against	Points
34	26	6	2	111	33	58

Steve Chalmers finished the season as top league scorer with twenty-three goals. The luckless Joe McBride scored eighteen times in only fourteen Championship outings. Had *he* seen the season out, Jimmy

McGrory's record of fifty goals in a league season (1935/36) might well have come under serious pressure. The man originally intended as Joe's striking partner rather than his successor, Willie Wallace, grabbed fourteen in twenty-one games. [In his Centenary history of the club, 'Celtic, A Century With Honour', Brian Wilson quotes Billy McNeill, that, in Jock Stein's estimation, McBride and Wallace together would potentially have formed the deadliest striking combination in the history of the Scottish game and maybe even in Europe. Sadly, the partnership lasted only two games.] Bobby Lennox weighed in with thirteen goals from twenty-seven appearances and Jimmy Johnstone bagged the same tally from twenty-six. Tommy Gemmell scored nine, including three penalties (he took over the spot-kick rôle following McBride's exclusion, Joe having himself converted three). Bertie Auld got seven, John Hughes six, Bobby Murdoch four and Charlie Gallagher two. The remaining two were own-goals, contributed by Bobby Wilson of Dundee and George Miller of Hearts.

Interwoven with this commanding league performance, the domestic cup competitions had all been won with consummate ease. The League Cup had produced a haul of thirty-five goals for, with only seven against, over ten games. The Glasgow Cup had yielded three impressive 4-0 victories, of which, the demolition of Rangers at Ibrox on 22nd August, 1966 has already been covered in detail. The semi-final against Queen's Park at Celtic Park on 10th October featured a Joe McBride double, supported by singles from Lennox and Gallagher. The November final versus Partick Thistle, also at Parkhead, fell on a Monday, just two days after Celtic had faltered by dropping their first league point of the season in the 1-1 home draw with St Mirren, *the only match they had failed to win outright up to that point*. Any fears of creeping vulnerability were swiftly dispelled as Lennox, with a 'hat-trick' and Chalmers ran up another fearsome foursome without reply. The triumphant Scottish Cup tally was twenty goals scored, for the loss of only three, all to Queen's Park in that mad March affair! Of the six games played (including the replayed semi-final against Clyde), the Celtic goal had remained comfortingly intact in all but *that one*.

It would be a hard act to follow! Knowledgeable fans, however, will know that, although not so spectacularly successful in an overall sense, the very next season was to produce even *more* impressive league statistics.

Attention was now firmly focused on Lisbon.

Chapter Six

Twin Peaks: Lisbon ..... and Madrid.

Over the intervening years, oceans of eloquence, a battery of benedictions and the whole gamut of superlatives have been deployed in the rightful lionising of the events of 25th May, 1967. Almost every living supporter must have seen the highlights a thousand times. It may well be beyond the wit of man to further embellish that most glorious chapter in the saga of our *Grand Old Team.* Let us, therefore, pause a moment instead, just to reflect on the distinctive flavour of those formative times.

The sporting world had exploded into that May with Muhammad Ali, the World Heavyweight Champion, being stripped of his title by all world boxing authorities over his steadfast refusal to be drafted for U.S. Army service in Vietnam. 'I ain't got no quarrel with them Viet-Cong!' was Ali's typically pugnacious retort. It was probably the most controversial episode in the gifted but fatally-flawed champ's tempestuous love-hate relationship with the American and indeed, world boxing fraternity.

The Eurovision Song Contest winner, barefoot Sandie Shaw's rather inane 'Puppet on a String', topped the pop charts for the first two weeks of the month before being displaced, thankfully, by an altogether more memorable anthem of the 'sixties, the Tremeloes' classic, 'Silence is Golden'.

Sean Connery, a celebrated Celtic fan, happily pictured with the team on the pitch while attending the zany Queen's Park cup match during a springtime visit home, was still, as Commander James Bond, the world's biggest box-office attraction. His latest film, 'You Only Live Twice', would be ***the*** *cinema hit of the year.*

The Light Programme, the Home Service and the fossilised B.B.C. image that went with them were about to be consigned to the dustbin of broadcasting history as 'Auntie Beeb' prepared to bow to changing times through the phased introduction of a range of more dynamic, digitally-dubbed channels. Radio One would duly herald in the new era on 30th September, announcing its arrival in style with the strident echoes of the Move's 'Flowers in the Rain' - and somehow the world would never be quite the same again.

In Glasgow and throughout the country, the *Summer of Love* had been preceded by a winter and spring of adulation. Celtic could do no wrong. They seemed to be invincible, their manager, infallible. Yet the magnitude of the task which lay ahead and the awesome reputation of Inter Milan might daunt the staunchest supporter and it is appropriate at this juncture to take stock and put the situation into perspective.

Inter had won the European Cup at their first attempt, in 1964, beating the great Real Madrid 3-1 in the Vienna final. Although they were already pioneering the dreaded defensive system known as the *Catenaccio Bolt*, devised by their Moroccan coach, Helenio Herrera, in which an auxiliary defender (in Inter's case, left-half and captain, Armando Picchi) patrolled the area behind the back four, 'bolting the door' against attacking intruders, it was, in essence, by no means a revolutionary idea. Uruguay had won the 1950 World Cup in Brazil, beating the brilliant and hot-favourite host nation in the final, using a similar 'sweeper' system. Likewise, roving centre-half, Ernst 'Clockwork' Ocwirk, had performed the role for the superb Austrian national side of the early 'fifties.

Inter's operation of the 'bolt' defence was superbly effective, ironically because they had such technically talented and skilful players. They exercised endless discipline and patience to frustrate opponents, allowing them to pour forward, inevitably exposing themselves occasionally at the back in the process. Absorbing all the pressure, Inter would then strike with lightning speed and precision to capitalise on those fleeting opportunities to break out of defence and exploit the vulnerable opposing rearguard. The tactic was deployed to perfection during the 1963/64 European Cup campaign, in which only Everton and Borussia Dortmund managed even to hold Inter to a draw away from the San Siro. The final victory over Real Madrid was achieved with remarkable ease, thanks in no small part to defensive blunders by the Spaniards, inadvisable against *any* opposition, against Inter, *fatal.* The championship was only retained in 1964/65 with some difficulty, beating Rangers along the way. Inter won the quarter-final first leg 3-1 in Milan, but lost 1-0 at Ibrox.Their subsequent semi-final victory over Liverpool was shrouded in controversy.The English Champions had taken a first-leg lead of 3-1 in a powerful display at Anfield and hopes were high south of the border that, at last, the Holy Grail of European club football was on its way to its 'rightful home'. However, Sassenach dreams were snuffed out as Inter turned the screw in front of their screaming, firework-throwing fans in the San Siro. Liverpool's aggregate lead was cancelled out, then Piero took questionable advantage of some dithering by Liverpool's bulky Scottish goalkeeper, Tommy Lawrence, affectionately known on the Kop as 'The Flying Pig'. Did someone say, 'affectionately'? Lawrence had beaten Piero to a through-ball and the Italian's momentum had carried him over the bye-line. Then, as the 'keeper repeatedly bounced the ball whilst pondering how best to clear his lines, the crafty attacker nipped round from behind, nicked the ball away and gleefully rammed it into the empty net. Liverpool complained vehemently that the goal was illegal on the grounds of ungentlemanly conduct (player returning to the field of play without the referee's permission, etc., etc.), but the plain fact was, they were caught out by a very sharp piece of opportunism, legal or otherwise. Anyway, as everyone knows, breaks in football tend to even out, and Liverpool themselves would benefit from a shameful refereeing decision in another European semi, *at Celtic's expense,* only one year on, as reported earlier.

While Inter struggled towards a second European Cup Final, then, Benfica were knocking opponents over like ninepins, beating Real 5-1 in the Estadio da Luz en route to a showdown with the clinical Italians. Unfortunately for Benfica, the final was scheduled for Milan, a home game for Inter. Although the Portuguese protested bitterly, there was no getting round the problem - they just had to make the best of it. In the event, Inter were unconvincing in the 'backyard' final and only won by dint of a speculative long shot by Brazilian winger Jair, which slipped under goalkeeper Costa Pereira's body in the appalling rainy conditions.

Season 1965/66 saw Inter well in contention again, but eliminated at the semi-final stage by Real Madrid, who were poised to claim their sixth title and with it, permanent retention of the original *L'Equipe* trophy. Though the Spaniards penetrated the Milanese defensive curtain just once in their own Santiago Bernabeu Stadium, it was enough for a first-leg lead and when Amancio extended their advantage in the return, it was all over for Inter. The best they could muster was a late equaliser - but it was too *late* and too *little!*

Such, then, was Inter's sinister pedigree - two wins and a semi-final defeat by the eventual champions out of three starts in the preceding three years. Despite all of which, the carefree attitude with which Celtic and their supporters approached the European Cup Final of 1967 is a matter of legend. In the eyes of Europe's football press and assorted pundits, the Italian form horses were red-hot favourites. *Of course,* it was somewhat grudgingly conceded, Celtic had forged a passing

European reputation of their own with their two recent runs to the semi-final of the Cup-Winners' Cup, but they had no real *stars,* no names to compare with the likes of Inter's Facchetti or Mazzola. They had done exceptionally well, but were now surely out of their depth. They were the corner shop to Inter's supermarket.

Nonetheless, in the run-up to the big day, it was Celtic who undoubtedly won the battle for the hearts and minds of the local Portuguese, and indeed of neutrals everywhere, hands down. They were the 'Apostles of Attack', the good guys who had ridden into town to shoot up the baddies and free the football world from the stifling oppression of *Catenaccio.* They had risen from the turn-of-the-century hovels of Glasgow's East End to savour the millionaires' playground of Estoril, had graduated from *The Poor Children's Dinner Table* to the chequered street cafés of Europe, without acquiring the attendant airs and graces. It was a fairytale in the making and Celtic were *The People's Champions* before a ball was kicked.

History records that Jock Stein trumped every effort of Helenio Herrera's to gain an edge for Inter. He ensured that Celtic were

Photograph courtesy of Evening Times/Herald

The Lisbon Motorcade sets off from Alexandra Parade led by the official Evening Times Hillman Imp, Sunday 21st May, 1967.

accorded training facilities at the Estadio Nacional on the eve of the game at the same time of day as the actual match, despite attempts by Inter to muscle in. He insisted on occupying the 'Home' bench during the game, not through pushiness but *by right,* as it had been allocated to Celtic - again despite the pressure of arriving to find Herrera already sitting there. The language barrier was no obstacle, as the 'Big Man' clearly conveyed to his counterpart the dire consequences which would certainly ensue if he did not shift - *pronto!* The unprecedented travelling support played a huge part in winning over the locals, spreading their native goodwill everywhere. They were good-natured, high-spirited, irrepressible, irresistible and how the Portuguese loved them.

Bertie Auld is generally accredited with the final touch of psychological one-upmanship by starting up a chorus of *The Celtic Song* in the tunnel leading to the pitch. *That* Celtic were 'gallus' - and the Italians didn't know what to make of it. Nevertheless, professional to the last, Inter still looked calm, detached and confident as these teams lined up for the biggest game in Celtic's going-on-eighty-year existence:

CELTIC :- Simpson; Craig & Gemmell; Murdoch, McNeill & Clark; Johnstone, Wallace, Chalmers, Auld & Lennox.

INTER :- Sarti; Burgnich & Facchetti; Bedin, Guarneri & Picchi; Domenghini, Cappellini, Mazzola, Bicicli & Corso.

Celtic began the game impressively enough, finding their men with accurate passes, but Scottish hearts were in mouths after only four minutes as Inter nearly scored in their very first attack. Mazzola set Corso free down the left and made a menacing support run to the near post. He met the winger's pulled-back cross on the six-yard line and Simpson was relieved to block the powerful downward header with his knees. Cappellini, following up, lobbed the ball back into the goalmouth, but Simpson clutched it cleanly and the lightning threat had passed. The early confirmation of Inter's ability to strike like a cobra was met firmly by a swift and encouraging Celtic reply. Craig had already hit the bye-line, but his final delivery had been poor. Now Lennox hared down the same flank and sent over a peach of a cross. Jimmy Johnstone, of all people, rose unchallenged on the penalty spot and bulleted a header which Sarti only just managed to fingertip over the bar! Back came Inter, though, and disaster struck in only seven minutes. Mazzola collected a pass inside his own half, wide on the right. Drifting left across the field, he released the ball with precision into the path of Cappellini, who had pulled Craig out of position in making a

Photograph courtesy of Evening Times/Herald

The airlift gets underway too. This super-confident group includes former Celtic left-back, 'President' Jim Kennedy (third from right).

complimentary scissors run across the Celtic eighteen-yard line. Inevitably, the Italian inside-man went down like the proverbial 'sack of tatties' as Craig tackled, clumsily rather than heftily. Referee Kurt Tschenscher of West Germany was in no doubt, pointing to the spot amid futile howls of protest from the massed green and white ranks on the terracing. A penalty it was!

Mazzola waited patiently until the fuss died down and coolly sent Ronnie Simpson the wrong way. 1-0! Hearts sank in the stadium and in television rooms across Scotland. This was exactly what everyone had dreaded, the unthinkable ... and pure meat and drink to the Italians. Surely, now, Inter would simply shut up shop and revert to their favourite game of cat and mouse.

Somehow, though, Celtic absorbed the sickening kick in the groin, roared back upfield and Sarti visibly flinched as he clutched a stinging right-foot drive from Bobby Murdoch. Two minutes later, Murdoch got another glimpse of goal and this time cracked a left-foot shot wide from the edge of the area. In their finest hour, Celtic were playing majestically and Bertie Auld came within a whisker of equalising. He ran diagonally across the Inter defence into the box and with the Italians expecting a pass, suddenly spurted clear and clipped a left-footer off the face of the crossbar. Something had to give, it seemed and on the half-hour mark, the flagging 'prima donnas' were living dangerously again. Their now-rattled defence failed to clear a cross from the right and Gemmell hit a vicious, swerving right-foot volley which Sarti deflected for a corner only by diving full-length across his goal.

Celtic sustained this pressure for the remaining quarter of an hour of the first half, but the fans had another heart-stopping moment to endure before the interval. Guarneri momentarily relieved the mounting siege on Inter's goal by simply hoofing the ball as far upfield as he could. Such was Celtic's dominance, there was no-one bar Simpson in their half of the park. As the veteran goalie ran fully ten yards outside his area to meet the ball, sudden danger flared as Domenghini bore down on him. Ronnie confounded everyone, maybe even himself, however, by waiting until the winger was almost on top of him, then 'calmly' back-heeling the ball to the frantically recovering John Clark. The 'keeper later explained his potentially suicidal action by saying he realised that if he had fluffed his kick, or if Domenghini had charged it down, then a goal would have been almost inevitable, so he elected to draw the attacker in and play the ball to safety. What composure under pressure! If the fans had shared it, we would all have been spared a severe bout of apoplexy.

As the teams trooped off at half-time, with Celtic still trailing 1-0 despite such domination, there was understandable anxiety inside the stadium and amongst the T.V. millions that the players might lose heart. However, Jock Stein was able to reassure them that they were doing everything right, save for one minor but vital point. He had continually drummed it into his team that the way to beat a packed defence was to *turn* it and his final, brilliant masterstroke of the season was just to reinforce that simple message. His dressing-room theme was the importance of creating positions for the cut-back. Subsequent events would demonstrate how attentively his men were listening.

Responding to the heroic first-half performance, the fans were quick to get behind the team, roaring encouragement as they reappeared. Any notion Inter may have had that the Scots would be discouraged was swiftly dispelled as the second period commenced. Celtic were convinced they had equalised after ten minutes. Bedin attempted a hitch-kick clearance which nearly decapitated Wallace as he challenged for a high, bouncing ball deep inside the Milan box. At first it seemed Herr Tschenscher had awarded a second penalty, racing into the area and pointing dramatically towards the spot. However, he had, in fact, given an indirect free-kick for dangerous play. Wallace tapped the ball to Lennox, only twelve yards out, but his shot was charged down. Gemmell pounced on the loose ball and fired through a ruck of players. The effort took an awkward deflection off his opposite number, Facchetti, past the wrong-footed Sarti. The goalkeeper displayed amazing agility by twisting himself on the ground and lunging after the diverted ball. He was judged to have clawed it back before it actually crossed the line, despite Stevie Chalmers's close attendance and insistence that the ball *had* gone over. At home and in the stadium, fans leapt joyously to acclaim the 'goal' but again had to swallow their disappointment.

Still Celtic stayed cool, refusing to panic as the minutes ticked agonisingly past and beckoning glory seemed to recede. Wave after wave of attacks continued to stretch the Italians to the full, but the line held. Then, as the sixty-third minute clocked up, Jim Craig pushed forward down the right yet again and laid the ball square across the eighteen-yard line to Murdoch. Unfortunately, suffering a 'dead leg', the half-back had to let the ball run to his left foot and was crowded out before he could shoot. Undeterred, Bobby dropped back to collect the ball again and arrowed a perfect pass wide, back to Craig, still well forward on the right. The right-back held his ground, inviting defenders to come to him. In response, two Italians were sucked away from their marking targets as Craig released the ball at precisely the right moment, pulling it back along the eighteen-yard line into the path of his full-back partner, Tommy Gemmell, arriving like an express train bang in front of the Inter goal. The next instant is one of those forever imprinted on the freeze-frame of the mind's eye of every Celtic supporter who witnessed it. Inter captain, Picchi, lunged towards Gemmell as if to block the coming shot, but, frankly, chickened out as big Tam made devastating contact. His right-foot drive thundered past the powerless Sarti's right hand and tore at the netting, leaving the beaten 'keeper desperately pointing accusing fingers at the retreating figures of Lennox and Wallace, either or both of whom may have been caught in technically offside positions as the Inter defence instinctively streamed out towards Gemmell. The appeals of the defiant man in black, who had repelled everything Celtic had thrown at him up 'til then, were in vain - even his own team-mates declined to take up the lost cause with the referee, trudging wearily back to the centre-circle, mutely conceding the inevitable. Inter were beaten and they *knew* it. They had ridden the storm for over an hour and almost entirely exhausted their reserves of mental and physical energy in the process. Those much-vaunted, sophisticated defensive tacticians had long since been reduced to booting the ball anywhere, simply to survive. Now they were spent and bereft of hope.

Even then, one man, Guillermo Sarti in the Inter goal, continued to play the game of his life, utterly refusing to capitulate. The very man Jock Stein had fingered as a potential chink in the Italian armour repeatedly pulled off breathtaking saves to defy Celtic long after his colleagues had thrown in the towel. In the seventieth minute, Gemmell again rampaged up the Celtic left, leaving hard-man Burgnich trailing in his wake. Auld's attempted shot from the full-back's cross was charged down, but the ball broke for Murdoch to cream a glorious left-foot volley from twenty yards. Ninety-nine times out of a hundred, such a shot would have billowed the rigging. This time, though, Sarti launched himself and turned the ball over the bar - another wonderful, heartbreaking save.

If ever a goalkeeper earned a lucky break, it was Sarti that day and he got it when he made just about his only direct mistake of the match with fifteen minutes remaining, misjudging a cross-cum-shot from Gemmell on the left touchline. The ball sailed over his head and rebounded into play from the junction of post and crossbar. The next ten minutes saw the 'keeper constantly involved in more frenetic action. First, he plucked the ball off Willie Wallace's head following a Johnstone cross, then he was required to beat out two shots in quick succession from Murdoch on the left side of his area.

As the game entered its last ten minutes, Inter survived their biggest scare yet. A low cross from Gemmell eluded the killing touch of a Celtic forward. Guarneri, beyond the back post, attempted to shepherd the ball back to Sarti, but as the pair of them hesitated, Wallace nipped in to steal it away. He had already sidestepped the 'keeper and was about to knock the ball into the unguarded goal when Sarti blatantly grabbed his leg and hauled him to the ground. *A stonewall penalty!* Astonishingly, Herr Tschenscher waved play on. We can only surmise that he was unsighted and judged Wallace to have accidentally fallen over Sarti's outstretched arm. Perhaps he felt the 'keeper deserved the benefit of any doubt there may have been in his mind over the incident. Whatever the reasoning, his leniency might have been very costly for Celtic and the goalkeeper's earlier good fortune was eclipsed by that outrageous let-off.

Although there were only about five minutes left to play, it was hard to imagine Inter holding out for extra time. Anyway, Stein had left his players in no doubt that they were a lot fitter than their Latin opponents and would consequently be much better equipped to cope with extended play, or even a replay on the Saturday, should that be the way of things. On the evidence of the first eighty-odd minutes, it would be impossible to argue.

The world will never know what might have come about had the sides still been locked at 1-1 at time-up, for, in the eighty-fifth minute, Celtic claimed the cup for Glasgow, Scotland and everyone ever connected with the club, right back to its spiritual roots in Ballymote, County Sligo, home town of founder, Brother Walfrid. Once again, Gemmell, so significant a player on the day, danced down the Celtic left and laid the ball back into the path of Murdoch, now very obviously favouring his left foot (he later disclosed that his right ankle had been injured in training and was heavily strapped for the match). 'Murdie's' low drive was probably heading wide of the far post until Stevie Chalmers staked his personal claim to Celtic immortality with his historic deflection, which caught everyone else flat-footed and left Sarti stranded, for the glory goal.

The remaining, interminable, minutes produced no further incident, but it all appeared to be too much for Jock Stein. As the referee checked his watch and glanced at his linesmen, the great bear-like figure rose from the Celtic bench and lumbered off down the track towards the dressing rooms. Even before he had reached the tunnel, it was all over.

A final whistle had never sounded so sweet, provoking a joyous invasion of fans in varying stages of serenity, some bordering on delirium. Hell-bent on paying homage at the very shrine of the latter-day miracle they had just beheld, they charged over the moat surrounding the pitch, which the Portuguese authorities had

Photograph courtesy of Evening Times/Herald

We've done it! Steve Chalmers wheels away after knocking in the Lisbon winner, totally ignoring Sarti's futile protests.

Photograph courtesy of Evening Times/Herald

Billy McNeill hoists the trophy in the pose that proclaimed Celtic to the world as Britain's first ever European Champions.

optimistically fancied would deter such an incursion. The fans' unrestrained delight was totally understandable, but, regrettably, their presence on the pitch, however benign and well-intentioned, was potentially dangerous, not only to themselves, but also to the very players who had done them so proud; and it meant there could be no collective presentation of the cup to the team and no lap of honour. *What a pity that was*, for no team ever more richly deserved such a tribute than Celtic at the Estadio Nacional in Lisbon on 25th May, 1967. Instead, captain Billy McNeill ran a draining gauntlet of well-wishers to accept the trophy alone, high on the terracing, proudly splendid in his exhausted isolation, savouring the moment, the zenith of a wonderful career, as he raised that huge cup aloft in historic pose.

It was a truly glorious feat and one which threatened to 'square the circle' by uniting the highly polarised football factions of Scotland. Celtic came home the next day to a tumultuous welcome, in which an estimated 200,000 people of every allegiance and none lined the route from Glasgow Airport to Celtic Park, where the squad paraded the European Cup before 60,000 rapturous fans. The club's achievement was officially recognised not only by the House of Commons, but also by the General Assembly of the Church of Scotland, which was in session in Edinburgh at the time. Enough said!

The country then held its breath to see if Rangers could go on to heap history on history - if they could beat Bayern Munich in the Cup-Winners' Cup Final in Nuremberg, then Glasgow would become the first city ever to provide the winners of *both* major European club competitions in the same year. Sadly, the Ibrox club could not complete that momentous double. Playing with a recognised strong-man half-back, Roger Hynd, at centre-forward, they lacked the subtlety of fire-power to penetrate the well-drilled Bayern defence although they matched the Germans in every other department. In what was virtually a home game for their opponents, Rangers took the tie to extra time before succumbing to a lobbed goal by right-half Roth, who, along with team-mates on the night Franz Beckenbauer, Sepp Maier and Gerd Müller, went on to form the nucleus of the great Bayern side of the mid-seventies. Of course, Maier, Beckenbauer and Müller all also won World and European Nations Cup medals with West Germany, while Roth himself went on to gain the rare distinction of scoring the winning goal in both major European finals. He sealed that double with Bayern's winner against St Etienne with a thunderous right-foot drive in the European Cup Final of 1976 at Hampden Park, which completed a 'hat-trick' of victories on the trot for the great Bavarian club.

So it was a case of, 'Hard luck, Rangers' ... but Celtic still had one more glamorous occasion in which to participate, one more glittering prize to attain in that sparkling *Season in the Sun*. At the outset, they had defeated their eventual successors as European Champions, Manchester United; along the way, they had overcome the champions of 1964 and 1965, Inter Milan; and now, as a grand finale, they had their prior commitment to provide the opposition in a testimonial match for the legendary Alfredo Di Stefano, against Real Madrid at the Bernabeu, on Wednesday, 7th June. Real, Celtic's immediate predecessors as Champions of Europe, would be desperate to show that *they* were still really the team to be reckoned with in Europe. A lot would depend on Celtic's attitude. If they treated it like a friendly and played the kind of exhibition football normally purveyed on such occasions, a determined Real would probably win, perhaps even humiliating them in the process and undermining

Photograph courtesy of Evening Times/Herald

Traffic chaos in London Road as the team bus arrives for the homecoming Gala Night at Celtic Park.

Photograph courtesy of Evening Times/Herald

Inside the stadium Jock Stein joins in the celebrations with the players and backroom staff. Left to right are Joe McBride, John Clark, Sean Fallon, Steve Chalmers, Stein and Jim Brogan.

Celtic's new prestige so soon after their Lisbon triumph. There was no real danger of Jock Stein allowing *that* to happen, though. He had his troops well and truly geared up for the job and once again, Celtic went out and did themselves and Scotland proud.

For the Madrid match, John Fallon replaced Ronnie Simpson in goal. Willie O'Neill came in at the left side of the mid-line, with John Clark moving to right-half, Bobby Murdoch to inside-right and Wallace replacing Chalmers at centre-forward. Real started as though they intended to teach the impertinent Scottish usurpers of their throne a salutary lesson, but Celtic weathered the initial storm and were soon dictating play in their customary manner. Tommy Gemmell simply took up from where he had left off in Lisbon, making two foraging runs up the left wing before cutting in for potshots at the Spanish goal. The second of these culminated in a mazy dribble past two defenders and a blistering right-footer which forced a great save out of the 'keeper. Later, John Fallon produced a remarkable one of his own when he slipped, but recovered to throw himself athletically across his goal and clutch, not just parry, a point-blank shot from inside-forward Serena. Minutes later, he tipped a long shot from the same player over the bar. It was clear by this time, however, that Jimmy Johnstone had decided to make it *his* night. The nominal star of the show, Di Stefano, had departed after a token appearance of fifteen minutes, to be replaced by Grosso, but 'Jinky' was weaving his magic all over the pitch and Real's defence just couldn't cope with him. He was buzzing around like a hyper-active midget, taking players head-on, skipping past lunging tackles with a drop of the shoulder or a deft side-step, an elusive *Will o' The Wisp* who simply could not be tamed. The wee man chose this match to give a rampant virtuoso demonstration of his uncanny talent. No other footballer in the world, of *that* or any other era, could match Jimmy's unique ability to apparently defy the laws of physics in relation to motion, acceleration and momentum. He could seemingly stop dead almost in mid-stride while running flat-out, or change direction and virtually turn *himself* inside-out, never mind his opponents. Above all, Jimmy had the indomitable spirit to courageously shrug off the vicious kicks and fouls which invariably came his way as the last resort of lesser players; and even in a prestige 'friendly', especially at that level, rugged defenders were just as loathe to be made fools of as at any other time. However, 'Jinky' capped a memorable display by laying the only goal of the game on a plate for his great pal, Bobby Lennox. The move started deep in the Celtic penalty area, where Real's Serena tried to be far too elaborate in engineering space for a shot at goal and was snuffed out by O'Neill and Murdoch, who slipped the

Photograph courtesy of Evening Times/Herald

John Fallon sees the ball over the bar in the Di Stefano testimonial as Bobby Murdoch stands guard in the goalmouth.

ball to Gemmell. Finding his favourite route up the left wing blocked, Tam switched the ball inside to Johnstone, lying in a deep inside-left position. Jimmy accelerated past one tackle, wrong-footed two defenders by turning abruptly infield, then slid an inch-perfect pass through the defence into the path of Lennox, who showed his appreciation by placing a sweet shot precisely into the net at the far post, beyond the reach of the advancing Hunquera. It was the last goal of Celtic's *Wonder Year* and one of the best. Its execution encapsulated the team's whole approach - calm, efficient defending, enterprising full-back and midfield play, individual brilliance of the highest calibre and blinding speed of thought and movement, all rounded off by absolutely lethal finishing. Willie Wallace should have added a second, having been presented with a clear shooting chance courtesy of Johnstone and Lennox once again slicing Real apart, but 'Wispy' blazed the ball hurriedly over the bar with his left foot. For the remainder of the game, Celtic, and Johnstone in particular, felt secure enough to finally turn on the exhibition stuff. By the end, the Spanish fans had taken wee Jimmy, 'The Flea', as they dubbed him, to their hearts and they gave him an ecstatic and thoroughly well-deserved ovation.

As the final whistle sounded, Johnstone was, fittingly, in possession of the ball, which he picked up and raised one-handed above his head in salute to a generous crowd who had come to see Celtic buried, but stayed to acclaim the new kings in the deposed monarchs' very own courtyard.

Epilogue

Just *how* good were the Celtic of 1966 and 1967? Comparisons are, of course, odious and greatness is a rare quality indeed. But let there be no doubt that the Celtic whose nucleus and heart were 'The Lisbon Lions' *was a truly great team* which deserves to be bracketed in history with all others of that ilk, whether before or since. Over those two years they not only defeated the European Champions of 1964, 1965, 1966 and 1968, but also, as a prelude to the infamous series of matches to determine the unofficial World Club Championship of 1967, they won a friendly match with the *then* World Champions, Peñarol of Montevideo, Uruguay, who had defeated Real Madrid 2-0 both home and away to win the title in October, 1966. Celtic turned on the Lisbon style in beating Peñarol 2-1 at Celtic Park in September, 1967, both goals coming from Wallace, with Spencer netting for the World Champs. Sadly, we can only speculate whether Celtic would have prevailed over Peñarol in Uruguay, had they remained South American Champions.

As it was, the new European Champions had to contend with Racing Club, who had, under the stewardship of the cynical Juan Carlos Lorenzo, coach of the Argentinian World Cup squad of 1966, kicked and spat their way to the South American title. Lorenzo's Argentina had been branded 'animals' by England boss, Alf Ramsey, following a stormy quarter-final at Wembley the previous year, an insult which still rankled in lingering resentment of the English. The South Americans seemed determined to avenge the calumny at Celtic's expense, failing to distinguish between England and Scotland. As a result, there ensued the most disreputable episode in Celtic history, in which, it has to be said, some Celtic players, admittedly under the most extreme provocation, played an unsavoury part.

The disgraceful events of those three matches have been minutely dissected and reported many times since and really have no place in this book of celebration. Let it suffice to say, it seems no mere coincidence that the self-same Juan Carlos Lorenzo brought further vicious intimidation and mayhem to Celtic Park seven seasons later in the notorious European Cup semi-final of 1973/74, when his Atletico Madrid set about kicking their way into the final. Thankfully, they got their come-uppance in Brussels, snatching defeat from the jaws of

Photograph courtesy of Evening Times/Herald

Twenty-five years on, the 'Lisbon Lions' were still a happy-looking bunch as Celtic's most famous team ever was honoured at a 'Silver Jubilee' Civic Reception at Glasgow City Chambers on 27th May, 1992.

victory when Bayern Munich grabbed a last-ditch equaliser before slaughtering them 4-0 in the replay.

Although many more seasons of spectacular success, tainted now and then by bitter disappointment, were to follow before the sun went down for a time on Celtic's horizon, none would supersede 1966/67 for sheer roller-coaster exhilaration, as the team scaled new heights, even by the standards of a club so accustomed to setting the pace. Its events enriched the lives of all who shared in them, are signposts for those in need of direction and stand as a beacon among beacons on the high ground of Celtic history.

Appendix

The Past is Prologue: The Epic Victories

As the writing of this book got underway, Celtic were in the doldrums, struggling through another fruitless campaign (1991/92). Languishing well adrift of the Rangers juggernaut in the league, the League Cup had already slipped away, rising hopes cruelly dashed at the quarter-final stage within the tight confines of Airdrie's Broomfield Stadium, without even the consolation of feeling hard done by on the night. Only the chase for a European place in season 1992/93 (ultimately gained rather embarrassingly through a political back door) and lingering, forlorn hopes of Scottish Cup glory remained for the long-suffering fans to cling to. Even the welcome respite of an overdue victory in the hugely-popular, though largely diversionary, indoor 'Tennents Sixes' was scant compensation for the prevailing dearth of success in the real game.

A sad, then, but not unfamiliar scenario to anyone with a sense of Celtic history, who will surely recognise in it echoes of the recurring slumps which have punctuated the streaks of soaring achievement so characteristic of the Celtic saga. And that's the moral of the story! For, while such familiarity cannot lessen the pain of persistant failure for those who care about the club, recognition of the pattern and its inherent promise of better things to come should help stave off depression and eliminate pointless recriminations. To the Celtic 'faithful', *particularly in the bad times,* a backward glance can be a source of both comfort and inspiration. Awareness of the rich heritage they share *with* and *through* the club should put even the most modest of presents into a more tolerable perspective and 'trail' the historical certainty of dazzling future horizons.

The Coronation Cup
(1953)

The late, crusty, Celtic Chairman, Sir Robert Kelly, always maintained that winning the Coronation Cup stood favourable comparison with any other single achievement as the club's greatest-ever feat, in his opinion bracketed even with the Lisbon pinnacle of 1967. It is easy to see why when you consider what a highly-improbable success it was.

With only the Scottish Cup of 1951 to show for their post-war domestic efforts (excluding the 'extra-curricular' St Mungo Cup, of which, more later) and having just finished a poor eighth in the League Championship immediately preceding the competition, it could be (and *was*) argued that Celtic scarcely merited their place in a tournament which was intended as a 'Battle Royal' amongst the cream of British football. Indeed, there were those who would have been happy to see the 'Bhoys' left out in the cold and *some* public comment was openly scathing of their inclusion. All of which was to make eventual triumph the sweeter!

A combination of 'political' sensitivity, historical precedent and most of all, economic common sense prevailed over narrow-mindedness and saw to it that Celtic took their rightful place amongst the country's élite — not so very different then from now, as it happens.

England fielded their newly-crowned League Champions, Arsenal, together with the previous two seasons' title-winners, Manchester United and Tottenham Hotspur, as well as the double F.A. Cup winners of 1951 and 1952, all-conquering Newcastle United. The Scottish contingent, over and above Celtic, comprised Rangers, Hibernian and Aberdeen. The 'Gers and Hibs had been League Champions and runners-up of 1952/53, while Aberdeen were only narrowly beaten by the Ibrox men in a replayed 1953 Scottish Cup Final. Celtic, by comparison, had been performing indifferently for some time and could only offer former glories in defence of their nomination for this British 'Clash of the Titans'. Added to the well-documented dressing-room unrest in the run-up to the competition, things did not augur well at all for captain Jock Stein and his men.

Perhaps lulled into a false sense of security by Celtic's inauspicious credentials, first-round opponents, Arsenal, rather undiplomatically 'went public' over their misplaced confidence, which simply made the humiliation of their demise at the hands of the Parkhead 'no-hopers' the more intense. The narrow 1-0 scoreline greatly flattered the arrogant Londoners on the day.

Next up were Manchester United, conquerors of Rangers, who fell 2-1, despite being as well-fancied to dump the Celts as Arsenal had been before them. Very few were laughing now!

In the other half of the draw, Hibernian had been performing their own rather less-unexpected heroics, seeing off Spurs and walloping Newcastle United 4-0, to set up a 30th May final which few, if any, would have dared predict and which spawned that immortal line in the imaginative Coronation Cup celebration anthem:

'. . . and oh, what a scene — the terracings were covered in banners of green!''

The power of that fine Hibs side, particularly up front with their 'Famous Five' forward line of Smith, Johnstone, Reilly, Turnbull & Ormond, made them the overwhelming favourites. However, marshalled by Jock Stein, prompted by the tireless and creative wing-half displays of Bobby Evans and John McPhail and bolstered by the inspirational goalkeeping of Johnny Bonnar, Celtic again excelled themselves. Willie Fernie, who had taken over from Charlie Tully on the left wing in the only personnel or positional change throughout the competition, played a blinder, more than once drawing the best out of Hibs 'keeper, Tommy Younger.

The gifted Fernie had a hand in the truly sensational opening goal which broke the deadlock in the twenty-eighth minute. Willie flicked the ball into the path of Neil Mochan, who bulged the net behind Younger with a first-time thirty-yard screamer out of the setting sun. It is doubtful whether the goalie even saw it!

Wounded pride drew the best out of Hibs thereafter and the match proved to be Bonnar's finest hour. Johnny had been under pressure to retain his position and moves had even been made to secure a replacement. That day, however, he was immense, particularly in the second half as Hibernian gave him both barrels. His gutsy display finally broke the Easter Road spirit and allowed Celtic to finish them off with a decisive second from Walsh, again via Fernie, a few minutes from the end.

In the finest fairytale tradition, cynicism had been discredited, faith vindicated, the underdogs had triumphed and honour had been restored. Perhaps the last word should be left once more to that eloquent Coronation Cup song:

'. . . just watch that the Celts don't step in!'

The Celts who *did* step in for the historic final were:

Bonnar; Haughney & Rollo; Evans, Stein & McPhail; Collins, Walsh, Mochan, Peacock & Fernie.

Charlie Tully must also be accredited for his contribution throughout the competition before being injured out of the final, not least for his skilful assist in setting up Bertie Peacock's glorious eighteen-yard drive for the decisive second goal against Manchester United.

The St Mungo Cup (1951)

Those misguided souls who *so* denigrated Celtic prior to the Coronation Cup must have had very short memories indeed! For, less than two years previously, the same Celtic had similarly flown in the face of prevailing form to underline their renowned cup-fighting tradition in snatching the distinctive St Mungo Cup from the clutches of the other fifteen Scottish First Division clubs of the time, not least those *six* who had finished above them in the preceding season of 1950/51.

The competition had been jointly organised by Glasgow Corporation and the S.F.A. as part of the *Festival of Britain* celebrations. You might reasonably expect such an event to be dignified by a suitably-prestigious, perhaps even specially-commissioned trophy — and in a curious sort of way, maybe it was. Not as you might think, though; for in an apparent penny-pinching exercise, the organisers saw fit to resurrect and refurbish an ancient yachting trophy, dating back to 1894! Its only tenuous link with football lay in its having been converted in 1912 to be competed for in a match between the Glasgow Police and Provan Gasworks.

This dubious pedigree was discovered when, after the ceremonial presentation by the Lady Provost in the Kelvin Hall, a silver handle, fashioned in the shape of a salmon (one of the emblems of the City of Glasgow), came away in the hand of an admiring Celtic official. This prompted closer investigation, ensuing indignation and eventual irate demands for a replacement. Happily, the Corporation never relented, for if they had, the Celtic trophy collection would have been forever shorn of one of its most elegant components and arguably its most interesting conversation piece. In any case, surely the intrinsic honour of *any* prize heavily outweighs its questionable calibre or integrity? But enough of the politics, what of the sport?

Despite their indifferent league display, Celtic had rediscovered their legendary knock-out touch to lift the 'Scottish' of 1951 and that rich vein of cup form spilled over into the 'St Mungo', battling through to the final against Aberdeen at Hampden on Wednesday, 1st August. Finding themselves two down (against the run of play) after half an hour or so was not as daunting for Celtic as you might expect. They had pulled back a previous two-goal deficit to win en route to the final and would just have to do so again. Incidentally, between the two Aberdeen scores, Celtic captain, Bobby Evans, took over in goal for ten or twelve minutes after 'keeper Hunter had suffered a head injury which had to be treated off the field.

'Comes the hour, comes the man', they say — in this case, none other than the incomparable Charles Patrick Tully. 'Cheeky Charlie' lived up to his monicker with an outrageous piece of gamesmanship to drag Celtic back into contention minutes from the interval. The bold 'Bhoyo' bounced a throw-in off Aberdeen defender Shaw's back for a corner and Sean Fallon got the first of a personal double from the flag-kick, taken by Tully himself.

The equaliser came early in the second half, again from centre-forward Fallon, leaving Charles Patrick to help clinch things by setting up a decisive and controversial winner for Walsh following one of his very own mesmerising dribbles, including a *wave-play-on* after being fouled *and* Aberdeen protests that he had allowed the ball to run out of play before crossing.

Jack Mowat, one of Scotland's best-ever referees, officiated in the see-saw final, for which Celtic lined up as follows:

Hunter; Haughney & Rollo; Evans, Mallan & Baillie;
Collins, Walsh, Fallon, Peacock & Tully.

The above match description amends the brief account in an earlier book, 'The Glory of the Green — The Celtic Trophies.' John Traynor is glad of this revising opportunity.

The Empire Exhibition Trophy (1938)

It was Celtic's Jubilee year and the year of the great *Empire Exhibition*, centred on Glasgow's Bellahouston Park. A happy coincidence, which gave Celtic the opportunity to chalk up the first of those national celebration victories which have given the club an unparalleled record in such one-off competitions.

Celtic, Hearts and Aberdeen disposed of Sunderland, Brentford and Chelsea respectively in the first round but a Scottish 'full house' was thwarted by Everton's success against Rangers. The crowds for the matches, all at Ibrox, were very healthy, as were attendances at the Exhibition itself.

Divers (2) and Crum got the goals which beat Sunderland in a replay after a goalless draw and it was Crum again who scored the only goal of the semi-final with Hearts. That was enough to set up a glamour final against a powerful Everton side which was packed with internationalists, notably the great Tommy Lawton of England, with his fearsome aerial power.

A crowd in excess of 80,000 rolled up for the showdown on 10th June. Lawton, as expected, was a constant menace but Joe Kennaway and the Celtic defence in front of him were equal to the task and the ninety minutes elapsed without any score. Early in extra time, centre-forward Crum grabbed the goal which destined the striking trophy, a silver and marble replica of the Exhibition Tower, for Celtic Park. Scoring in every round was a sterling feat, well-deserving of a place for Crum in the Celtic *Hall of Fame*.

Legendary winger Jimmy Delaney later recalled the Exhibition Trophy team as the greatest he ever played in. According to Bob Kelly, the forward line was years ahead of its time, interchanging instinctively in an era when formal tactical coaching was unheard-of.

That front line led the following Celtic eleven to glory on 10th June 1938:

Kennaway; Hogg & Morrison; Geatons, Lyon & Paterson;
Delaney, MacDonald, Crum, Divers & Murphy.

The Glasgow Exhibition Cup (1902)

This spectacular testament to the silversmith's art was originally the property of Rangers Football Club, who had won it in an eight-club Scottish tournament to mark the *Glasgow International Exhibition* of 1901. A bruising, controversial final against Celtic had produced the kind of acrimonious aftermath which has been sadly characteristic of such occasions over the years.

In an altogether more desirable atmosphere of harmony and goodwill, the 'Old Firm' came together again the following year in a foursome with Sunderland and Everton to play a mini-tournament in support of the victims of the dreadful Ibrox Disaster of April 1902. Dozens were killed and hundreds injured when a terracing collapsed during the Scotland/England international. The competition was inevitably elevated into a sort of British Championship by the press of the day and Rangers saw fit to raise the stakes and reflect the hyped-up status of the event by offering their Exhibition Cup as a permanent prize.

It just *had* to be a Celtic/Rangers final and so it proved, as Celtic disposed of Sunderland, while Rangers knocked out Everton, leaving the Glasgow rivals to re-contest the trophy they had so recently disputed. In his book, 'The Story of the Celtic', Willie Maley recalls the confrontation as an epic double-header on 17th and 19th June, with Celtic winning through a third goal deep into extra time after a 2-2 draw.

Celtic enjoyed a much more emphatic victory over the 'Light Blues' a couple of months later in another match in aid of the Disaster Fund. There was no trophy on that occasion, only prestige and medals sponsored by Bovril being at stake as Celtic thumped the 'Gers 7-2, helped by a 'hat-trick' from Jimmy Quinn.

The Victory in Europe Cup (1945)

The war years were bleak ones for Celtic on the trophy front, yielding only the Glasgow Cup of 1940/41 and the Charity Cup of 1942/43. This was an era in which it was fashionable for clubs to field guest stars who happened to be handily stationed under wartime emergency conditions. Celtic never took the advantage of this provision that most of their rivals did, in the process depriving several personalities of the opportunity to realise their ambition of donning the hoops and to a degree explaining the lack of honours over the period.

The V.E. Cup was a device of the Glasgow Charity Cup Committee to celebrate the cessation of hostilities and raise funds for war charities and the invitation went out to Celtic and Rangers to contest the commemorative event. Rangers declined, leaving Celtic in opposition to stand-ins, Queen's Park, at Hampden Park on 9th May.

In the days before penalty shoot-outs, more imaginative, if less dramatic ways were found to decide drawn matches. When the teams were locked at 1-1, Celtic were awarded the cup on account of having forced one more corner than Queen's Park.

The occasion, then and the elegant silverware which dignifies it, are perhaps worthier than the manner of achievement. Nonetheless, the Victory in Europe Cup is rightly aligned with those other 'landmark' trophies which set Celtic apart from all other clubs in these islands.

The team which recorded the hairsbreadth V.E. victory was:

Miller; Hogg & McDonald; Lynch, Mallan & McPhail; Paton, MacDonald, Gallacher, Evans & McLaughlin.

Bobby Hogg and Malcolm MacDonald were survivors of the great Empire Exhibition team.

The League Cup Final (1957)

Hampden Park, 19th October 1957
Celtic 7 Rangers 1

Though not of the same *historical* nature as the above occasions, the '7-1' League Cup Final still has enormous emotional significance in Celtic folklore and as such, was, indeed, an *Epic Victory.*

Quite simply, nothing can be said that hasn't been said before about this result, *the* most famous scoreline in post-war Celtic history and still a record score for a national cup final in Scotland.

The immortal '7-1' team lined up as follows:

Beattie; Donnelly & Fallon; Fernie, Evans & Peacock; Tully, Collins, McPhail, Wilson & Mochan.